Reviews for *Courageous Auditing*

Insightful, reflective and thought-provoking read for both emerging and established quality system Auditors. Kathy challenges you to think beyond compliance to the space of VALUE and challenges auditors to evolve and step up.

—Katrina Johnson, Director, New Sky Consulting, Australia

Courageous Auditing provides a blend of Kathy's years of experience and observations as an assessor backed up by research and other's data. Kathy provides insight for people contemplating 'becoming an auditor' or in the early stages of professional development and the potential to truly make a difference for organisations that are audited.

—Suzanne Le Huray, General Manager, HDAA Australia

This is a courageous effort by the author to begin the important conversation of 'how an auditor should be in this changing world'. *Courageous Auditing* extends the prevailing model of 'audit'. It proposes a professional way of working, challenging all auditors to rethink their role and consider how they can genuinely advance the organisations they work with. I recommend this book to all auditors, old and new.

—David Hamer, Managing Director, HDAA Australia

I believe every upcoming auditor should read this book so they can learn and know what the requirements of being a 'good' auditor are. There is responsibility in being a catalyst for change and value adding, especially in services that were struggling.

—Brian Amos, Quality and Compliance Advisor, Queensland

This book is the 'go to' book for auditors and anyone who wants to hold an attitude of growth and lifting of standards in business and also in life.

—Lyne Mear, Chief HR Manager, Mear & Associates

A successful business audit requires two qualities – Leaders willing to learn and an experienced courageous auditor willing and capable to find the opportunities for improvement. Kathy Rees' book takes the auditing part to the top level of performance.

—David Stannard, The Vision Guy®, Author and Founder of Paradise Rescued

COURAGEOUS
AUDITING

Beyond compliance – towards being a catalyst for change

Kathy Rees

i.e.

First published 2020 by Kathy Rees

Produced by Indie Experts P/L, Australasia
indieexperts.com.au

Copyright © Kathy Rees 2020

Cover design by Daniela Catucci @ Catucci Design
Edited by Kaaren Sutcliffe
Internal design by Indie Experts
Typeset in 11.5/15.5 pt Minion Pro by Post Pre-press Group, Brisbane

A catalogue record for this book is available from the National Library of Australia

ISBN 978-0-6489581-0-9 (paperback)
ISBN 978-0-6489581-1-6 (epub)
ISBN 978-0-6489581-2-3 (kindle)

Disclaimer:

For Brian, who showed me the way.

CONTENTS

TO THE READER

Because I audit extensively in and across Australia's community sector, the experiences offered in this book are derived from what I have observed over many years. I do not presume to know what auditors working in other sectors or in other countries will experience. However, I am hopeful that these auditors might also gain some insights into some of the ways they, too, can improve their practice.

Having said that, the goal of this book is to guide you to think about and amplify your strengths and knowledge – even beyond attaining the position of being a Lead Auditor. *Courageous Auditing* is a book to encourage you on your journey of discovery as an auditor, as well as to open your mind to consider what you could do in order to make a valuable difference as a professional in this field.

This book can be read at whatever stage you are at, for example:

> If you are thinking about becoming an auditor and don't know what this really means in practice.
> If you have just completed the Lead Auditor course and don't know what to do next.

> ➤ If you have been a Lead Auditor for some time and wonder if this is all there is.
> ➤ If you are wanting to reflect on your auditor role to look at ways to improve what you are already doing.

Each chapter presents a different aspect of the auditor's journey. At the end of each chapter there are questions to encourage you to reflect, recognise and consider areas you might want to delve into and know more about.

This is your journey: one that will unfold as it should for you. If you have an open mind and want to explore further ways to be a courageous auditor, I offer you a challenge: from now on, step back and look at your auditing role in a different way. Commit to considering ways to provide far more value and insights in the way of service to the organisations and businesses you audit. Ask for feedback, extend your own knowledge and practice as much as you can, and continue your learning. This is a lifelong practice, one that only starts when your initial training concludes.

If you do any of that, then this book will have served its purpose.

Kathy Rees

to become a Lead Auditor. Apart from refining their technical skills and competencies, it is not clear how would-be auditors understand and appreciate that they will need to extend their own attitudes, beliefs and abilities to enhance their auditing role over time. Auditing is not just about developing and extending technical ability: it is about having the courage to recognise that the auditor's personal attributes, baseline beliefs and intent can make – or break – any audit experience.

Why is this important? Over the past decade, many people have found that no-one, in fact, actually talks about what is involved in auditing as a career or profession. There is scant information available to explain what people need to be aware of before they even consider training as an auditor. Certainly, little is visible for people to help them to consider their career beyond finishing the course and commencing in their role as either an internal or external auditor.

Usually, people become an auditor because they are interested in compliance and better practice or they have seen the benefits associated with being able to demonstrate continual improvement within organisations. For some people, auditing is a logical progression after their redundancy or as a contribution they can make to society during their retirement. In some cases, people become auditors because someone they know said they would be 'good' at auditing. Regardless of how people become auditors, this is a profession that can add significant value to organisations, businesses and the sectors that are not only required to meet designated standards but want to demonstrate best practice over time.

To undertake a meaningful and courageous auditing role requires auditors to not only understand and refine their own potential but also see the potential for growth in the organisations and businesses that they audit, regardless of the sector in which they are operating. In recent years, leading financial auditing firms have been exploring the idea of urging auditors to 'step up' and acknowledge the requirement to develop more in-depth skills and tools that add value to businesses and organisations. Frequently, the focus of these firms has been on what is required for the decade ahead and how the auditing profession itself should develop in order to be relevant to a vastly changing business environment.

However, this level of expectation does not appear to be as clear in other auditing arenas, including Australia's community service sector. This sector includes many different service types, such as general health, mental health, disability support, youth services, child safety and protection, advocacy, employment, domestic violence and women's services, as well as neighbourhood centres (amongst others). These arenas all require start-up and scheduled certification and accreditation audits to operate. From what I have seen, there does not appear to have been any particular call to action or expectation that external auditors operating across this sector would provide anything more than what is currently delivered by a Lead Auditor. But think about what would happen if it was expected that every auditor operating in this sector was actively developing and refining their audit approach to deliver maximum value. What a difference this would make: not only for the organisations and businesses striving to meet the needs of a broad clientele, but for the individuals requiring these services as well! Similarly, considered audit improvements that add value to individuals and the services that support them could also have a flow-on, upwards effect on government agencies that fund these services and organisations.

Consider the ways auditors could demonstrate that they are improving their practices to address a rapidly changing world that is affecting the businesses and organisations that they audit so that audits are seen to be a valued resource instead of a function that is commonly viewed as a 'necessary evil'!

Qualifying as a Lead Auditor is actually the beginning of your auditing journey. From that point onwards, you have so many opportunities to make a real difference, not only to the organisations, services and businesses you audit, but also to clients and the broader community over time.

1.

THE OTHER SIDE OF AUDITING

One isn't necessarily born with courage, but one is born with potential. Without courage, we cannot practice any other virtue with consistency. We cannot be kind, true, merciful, generous or honest.

(MAYA ANGELOU)

On the other side of auditing, where this all began

My journey to become an auditor commenced innocently enough. In the year 2000, I was a contracted trainer for a large Registered Training Organisation, travelling throughout southern Queensland to deliver accredited training courses to staff working for small as well as large community services. During one training contract, I was about to start the third session when one of the staff quietly asked, *'Kathy, what are your thoughts about people with disability being fed bread and water?'* This immediately caught my attention. I asked, *'What do you mean?'* Over the next twenty minutes, I heard about the instructions staff were expected to follow when people with disabilities did not respond to directions given to them by staff or the service managers.

As the staff member explained what she was expected to do when people with disabilities were frustrated, expressed their needs angrily or would not respond to directions, the other staff added details of their experiences. Feelings of inadequacy and concern were shared as they talked about their reactions to the bread and water regime: the punishment meted to clients for actions that occurred earlier in the day.

However, not every person with a disability understood the punishment and, in fact, the person being punished had often forgotten what had happened earlier in the day. As a result, when they were presented with bread and water for their evening meal, they reacted to not receiving the same meal they could see other people eating. This, in turn, resulted in further punishment and, generally, an escalation of behavioural responses.

The staff said they didn't understand why they were expected to do this to people with disabilities, but the managers were adamant that this was the required practice when people with disabilities 'misbehave'. By the end of the twenty minutes, all of the staff involved in the training session were nodding and saying that this was standard practice.

Several people commented on the expression they could see on my face. I was dismayed and saddened by what I was hearing, not only for the people with disabilities, but also for the staff. I said that I would need to take some action by speaking to the manager as well as to the contact staff at the Registered Training Organisation who had engaged me for this work. It was immediately apparent to me that while the service was signing staff off as being competent for the completion of previous units, the actual practices that staff were instructed to deliver and were talking about contrasted with the expectations of the training course.

While walking to the manager's office, I thought about my own experiences in addressing situations where abuse and neglect had occurred or were alleged to have occurred. From the fallout from sexual assault experienced by my daughter who is a quadriplegic, blind and unable to speak, the active discrimination from mainstream service providers experienced by young homosexual men with traumatic brain injuries, the vulnerability of women with disabilities when they experience sexually inappropriate comments from their support workers, and the impact on adults with an intellectual disability when their parents actively steal from them. I had seen and heard a lot, not only in my role as a service provider, but also in my advocacy work. However, none of the students knew about that. What they heard from me were a lot of references about human rights, and professional and accountable service delivery practices. These references complemented the content in the accredited qualification on disability support work that they were undertaking at the time.

My discussion with the manager went badly. When I explained that the practice of punishing people with disabilities in this way had gone out of vogue a long while ago and was, in fact, in breach of Australia's disability legislations as well as human rights instruments, the manager told me that I was being 'ridiculous' and that these people 'deserved what they got'. I said that I would leave the site and report what I had been told to the authorities, which I did. First, to Queensland's Community Visitor Program, and then to the Registered Training Organisation to whom I was contracted. It transpired that other complaints had recently been made about this service and the Queensland Police Service had become involved. But to my dismay, senior officials managing the Registered Training Organisation told me that I had cost them a lot of money and they would do all they could to destroy my reputation. Clearly, my contracted work with them had finished!

Next steps

At the time, my response was to look at commencing my own Registered Training Organisation, one that would operate from a position of integrity and professionalism and be focused on training and assessment practices designed to escalate workers' knowledge and skills when supporting people with disabilities. Within a matter of months, I had collated and developed the necessary documents to get this started. First of all, though, I found out that I would need to take my fledgling Registered Training Organisation through its first audit in order to attain accreditation. This audit would be an assessment of my company's capabilities to not only manage this type of business but also provide professional and relevant training materials and processes to prospective students.

First audit experience

On the day of this first audit, I was incredibly anxious. All of a sudden, I was on the spot, no more talking about what needed to be done, but time for action and for other people to review what I planned to do.

The auditor came to my office and spent some time trying

to allay my concerns and fears. She reviewed the documents I had supplied and listened to the reasons I was commencing down this pathway. She said that this was the first stage of a long journey and that I would see a lot of change in my thinking and practice as time went by. While I felt like I was showing her I was calm and in control, the reality was I felt sick in my stomach and really just wanted the whole audit to go away.

However, the day went on and during the closing meeting the auditor provided some very positive feedback about my approaches as well as some constructive ideas for where I could make improvements. She explained that she had to prepare a report about what she had seen and provide this to her managers who would also review her evidence. She explained that I would hear the outcome in due course.

Following this initial audit, I didn't hear anything for quite a while from the certification body. I had just about given up hope when I received the message confirming my success while in Mt Isa delivering an information session to families about supporting people with disabilities to live independently. I had made this happen for my severely disabled daughter in 1994 and I was providing information to these families about how they could do the same. After some quiet celebrations, I returned home to start my journey of providing training for people interested in Certificate III or IV in Disability or Diploma of Management qualifications.

Actions following that first audit

In the years between the first audit for my registered training organisation in 2002 and the subsequent audit five years later,

I continued to research best practices in the delivery of support to people with disabilities living elsewhere in the world and incorporated this research into updated training materials. I set high standards, not only for the support practices, but also for the students who undertook my courses. It was inspiring to see the 'a-ha' moment for a student, the moment when the content clicked for them and they could see the link between what they were learning and the supports they were providing to people with disabilities. Of course, I was also seeing some students who simply saw the acquisition of the certificate as a way of continuing their employment and meeting their own needs. Some people didn't want to know any more than the minimum needed to get a job.

Throughout the training program, I also worked closely with the supervisors and managers of these organisations while the in-house training course was underway. We often saw students grow and develop additional skills and deeper appreciation for their roles in the lives of people with disabilities. Conversely, it also didn't take long to see which students may not be a good fit with the organisation, or who were not suited to this role.

Developing my own skills

I continued to refine my thinking about the practice of training and assessing students during this time. After meeting with a student who wanted to use his Certificate IV to enter university, I decided that I, too, needed to continue to develop my knowledge about training as well as in leadership and organisational management practices. This meant undertaking master's studies in organisational development and training, with the latter stages of this qualification being used for research that led me down the pathway of PhD studies.

I was immersed in furthering the skills and knowledge of my students too and provided many opportunities for people to consider not only the current environment for the disability sector, but also what might lie ahead. At the same time, in my consulting work and in the journal articles I was reading, the frustrations of people with disability and their family members were gradually becoming more apparent. Frustrations were being shared about not being involved in service delivery practices that directly affected them, being left out of funding discussions and, in some cases, discovering that their allocated funds had been spent by the service provider even though no support had been provided during the year.

Advocacy services championing the rights of people with disabilities were actively addressing these issues, and international research was vocal about the right of people with disabilities to be in control of their lives. The readings I provided to my students included information about what was happening across the Australian and international disability sectors as well as information about person-centred practices, human rights, business practices and professional communication skills.

Many students told me that being informed helped them to be more knowledgeable about how to manage a range of difficult situations in their work. The information also helped them to understand and appreciate the impact of their role on people with disabilities. From the feedback I received from the students, as well as from their managers throughout each course, it appeared that the readings were often the only way students received this level of information.

Preparing for the second Registered Training Organisation audit

By 2007 when the second audit of my Registered Training Organisation was due, I was in a very different place to the earlier audit experience. I had attended a number of Registered Training Organisation information-sharing meetings where the upgraded standards were examined in some depth. While these meetings helped me to be more prepared for the next audit, I quickly realised that I was not the only one who worried about what it would bring!

In the months prior to the second audit, I again reviewed the policies and procedures I used for training and assessing students along with the training materials I had developed from scratch. These materials comprised a learner guide, an assessment guide and a selection of readings for each topic. The intent of the materials was to help students to reflect on their progression from commencement through to completion of the unit topic – hopefully during the unit they had learned something that they didn't already know.

The majority of the students provided serious reflections upon their completion of the units, but I had also kept copies of some funny reflections that a number of students had made about the broader state of their lives. For example, when asked what they had learned since the commencement of the unit, comments were often made about how the use of the respectful communication principles could also be usefully employed by their children or their ex-husbands!

I also received feedback about ways the materials could be improved. Some students had expressed frustration about the way I asked questions in a series instead of one at a time, which led me to modify the reflection exercises that were a component of the overall assessment.

The second audit commences ...

On the day of the second audit, I felt quietly confident about my preparations, yet anxious and sick in the stomach at the same time. This Registered Training Organisation was my 'baby', something I had built up from nothing.

The auditor sat down opposite me before bringing out a swathe of paperwork. He asked me some standard questions about the background of the company before commencing his audit. I had no real idea about what to expect, seeing as the standards had changed in the months preceding this audit and the auditor was from the Australian Government, instead of the previous process which was overseen by the state government. I just hoped it would all go well.

Second audit surprises

The audit process went smoothly throughout the morning, with the auditor looking at a sample of the training materials as well as reviewing the policies and procedures that complemented the various indicators. It was challenging to realise that the wording of one sentence in one procedure could result in a non-conformity for an entire standard. I realised that the auditing world was very different to what I had experienced five years before.

Apart from the non-conformity due to a poorly constructed sentence, the morning went well until the auditor asked if he could see the management meeting minutes. After some initial surprise about this request when it was obvious that my company had only one director and currently no other staff, my response was: '*I would really like to help you with this but the reality is I am the sole director of the company and, no, I don't have management meeting minutes. There is no point in having these sorts of meetings with myself. To be honest, I talk to myself quite a bit and then answer myself with some very reasonable responses which I think sound quite plausible. No, I don't write these conversations down as minutes. I put them in the continuous improvement register because, most often, what I am talking about to myself are really ways to make improvements to the content of training materials or to company practices, that sort of thing. I think me talking to myself and answering myself sort of sounds quite nuts, but it actually really works as you can see by looking at the register and how the entries translate into improvements to the materials.*'

The auditor was taken aback, and then apologised. He said that he mostly audited large TAFEs, not small entities such as mine, and had asked this question from habit. He said that the register would 'have to do', even though the standards were not seeking continual improvement at the time.

Reflections on the second audit

As he worked through the audit checklists during the afternoon, I had time to reflect on my usual approach to managing new situations, such as this one. My preferred approach is to work things out as I go along and to look at the 'big picture' for opportunities and new ways of approaching a situation, which works well most of the time.

However, when I started to see the standards were a lot more involved than what I had previously experienced, I knew I would have to prepare in a very different way. Operating and managing the training organisation had taught me a lot of things about 'dotting the i's and crossing the t's'. This meant not only understanding the big picture of running a company in the registered training space, but also making sure all of the detail was covered at the same time. I could see that there would be unpleasant consequences if I did not attend to the detail, particularly in areas such as financial and reputational damage, with a lot of worry and anguish on my part to repair this sort of damage. My thinking was along the lines of Benjamin Franklin's quote:

*An ounce of prevention
is worth a pound of cure.*

Concluding the second audit

At the end of the audit, the auditor said that he only needed a day to go through what he had thought would take two to three days. He had seen enough. His concluding comments in the closing meeting focused on the attention he could see given to the standards the company was addressing as well as the high expectations for students as a result of undertaking my courses. He then recommended a further five-year audit cycle because the training organisation was not deemed to be a high risk. He explained that some Registered Training Organisations were audited every one to two years, based on their size and scale of operations as well as perceived risk. In his opinion, my Registered Training Organisation was well run and did not require regular audits.

To be honest, I thought this was a good outcome, but I rapidly came to see that five years is a long time in the lifespan of a training organisation. A lot of things can change quickly in that period, not least of which might include the implications associated with changes to the standards, financial implications associated with the ebbs and flows of student intake cycles, and the need to keep abreast of sector requirements with training practices. Given my strong focus on continuous improvement and the conversations I was having with other colleagues, I realised there was also the potential risk associated with engaging staff and contractors who might not fully understand or appreciate the focus I had on the delivery of training or the attention to detail in completing the work in the timeframes I required. This required further work on my part to ensure my Registered Training Organisation was as robust as possible.

Applying my audit experience in a new venture

The next audit of my Registered Training Organisation was not due until 2012. However, in 2011 I started another company to provide government funded supports to my disabled daughter. Establishing this company involved negotiating with the government agency responsible and responding to a series of entry criteria before the government would consider any form of service agreement or provision of funding. My learnings from my two audit experiences came in handy here.

One of the entry criteria questions focused on conflict of interest. To start with, I didn't respond to this, as I did not see that

I would have a conflict of interest with myself or for what I was doing for my daughter. The company, as far as I was concerned, was there to provide a foundation for her support and my role in the company was clearly about making sure the foundation was strong and solid so that she could live her best life, regardless of whether I was in the company or not.

However, reflecting on my training organisation audit experience, I realised that this would not be how external auditors would see it. After a rapid Google search, I was able to provide a Conflict of Interest Policy. This was what was needed to progress the application through the entry criteria and onto the first service agreement for my daughter's support.

Learning about a different set of standards

As I entered this new service agreement environment, I closely monitored the ways the standards were being implemented for the sector and thought the best way to be across what was required was to thoroughly research what the standards said and meant. I confess to thinking at the time that the best way for my company to provide the supports my daughter required was to be 'in the game' and to demonstrate what best practice is from the ground up.

Initial audits for this company were met with surprise from the auditor: surprise that I had covered what the standards require in the policies and procedures as well as in practice. My daughter's staff had embraced the truth of person-centred practice and could provide many examples of what this looked like in action. As a result, the audits did not result in any suggested improvement actions or observations, something the auditor said was highly unusual.

Around this time, I was asked to consider being an auditor. I had never thought of myself in this type of role. Understanding quality practices and having high standards – about what my training organisation should provide, as well as what the service for my daughter should demonstrate – was one thing. Systems thinking also made sense to me, but actually *being* an auditor? I was not sure, but I committed to becoming qualified as an auditor. I had no real idea about the mechanics of auditing and I realised I would need to know a lot more before stepping further into this world.

Lead Auditor training

Once I had made the decision to become an auditor, I searched for training programs that would address the basic requirements. I discovered that there were ISO (International Organization for Standardization) standards for the profession of auditing, and that qualifications were attainable through a range of organisations such as TAFEs, adult education service providers and some of the large management consultancy firms. The best starting point seemed to be to complete a Lead Auditor training course in quality management systems. These courses covered the principles and technical requirements for becoming either an internal or external auditor. The people I had met with explained the training program was the first step. Once completed, I could apply to become a third party, external auditor with the certification body they represented. They explained that there was a structured and orderly internal orientation process that also needed to be completed before I could become a fully-fledged Lead Auditor. But first things first, I thought.

The Lead Auditor training program saw me become immersed in the world of auditing, not only for human services standards, but also for other industries and sectors. It seemed to me that most of the people attending the training had had some form of internal auditing experience, mostly from a management or employee perspective. There were no other attendees who were business owners and had also been required to take their companies through audits. I was the only one with experience of the 'other side' of auditing.

Each day saw the gradual unfolding of the tasks and responsibilities a Lead Auditor assumes in an audit. We progressed through topics related to initiating and preparing for an audit, managing audit programs, conducting onsite audit activities, as well as conducting post-audit activities and reporting on the audit findings.

During the exercises, I struggled to only see one way of responding to the situation in front of me, even though this appeared to be what the training program required. So much of my life involved the many colourful shades of grey, not just those of black or white, and I thought at the time that being an auditor would thrust me into situations where many different possibilities would become apparent.

It was only later that I realised the training program was my first experience of having to comply with a system that required evidence of meeting pre-determined outcomes. I didn't realise that the Lead Auditor training program was simply the first step into a new world: so much more was to follow. But I didn't know that then and no-one talked about what was ahead.

Reflections

What was your first experience with auditing? How did you feel before the audit started?

....

....

....

....

What role did you have in that first auditing experience? Were you the auditor or a representative of the organisation being audited?

....

....

....

....

What differences in thinking/feeling do you think people might experience depending on whether they are either the auditor or the organisational representative?

....

....

....

....

If you have attended Lead Auditor training, recall your thinking about the training course you attended. Did it address what you expected? Were there any surprises in the course content? What did you take away from this training? Is there anything else the course could have covered but didn't?

....

....

....

....

....

....

In what ways did the Lead Auditor training help you to understand the wide array of standards that might be applicable to your auditing work?

....

....

....

....

....

....

2.

STARTING LIFE AS AN AUDITOR

Two roads diverged in a wood and I —
I took the one less traveled by,
And that has made all the difference.

(ROBERT FROST)

Where auditors start

While I commenced my journey as an auditor following a discussion with people looking for a person with existing credibility across a range of community networks, other people enter the field of auditing in very different ways. Some people do their research first before switching from one work role to the auditor role.

Some people find it difficult to find other work, so they look to auditing as an alternative in the meantime. Other people actively look at auditing as a way to give back to a sector or make improvements in a field where the quality of services may not appear to be that important to those providing them or as strong as it could be.

Regardless of how they come to their auditing role, most people take the time to do some or all of the following before commencing their journey. Reflecting on my own experience, here are some suggestions to consider:

> Honestly review your skills and attributes relevant to becoming an auditor. Research[1] based on a survey addressing the evolving role and processes of audits highlighted the requirement for auditors to address particular skill sets such as:
>   - experience in the client's industry
>   - investigative skills
>   - understanding data and analytics
>   - communication skills
>   - critical thinking and judgement.

> Talk with people who have been auditors for at least three to five years. These people can help you to understand what their work actually entails, what a standard day looks like, what they get paid, what happens when there is travelling involved, and what they enjoy and dislike about what they do. Discussions with existing auditors can provide a clearer picture about what you can expect when you become an auditor.

> Review your previous experience to see where you could be best placed as an auditor. Various sets of standards are used for different sectors and business functions, so it is helpful to consider which of these standards best match the type of experience you may already have. If your experience doesn't match, you may find the onsite audits challenging with clients who may rapidly ascertain your lack of industry experience.

➤ Examine your approach to learning. The reality is that
auditors cannot afford to stop learning and refining what
they know. The fact that updates to standards, guidelines
and technology occur on a regular basis is important
to understand. Some industry standards are clear that
auditors should not undertake auditing work that is
beyond the scope of their qualifications, knowledge and
expertise.

➤ Be aware of your personal approaches and biases towards
managing change. This is important because change is
one of the constants in this environment.

➤ Honestly appraise how you prefer your workday
to operate and flow. Audits are fast paced, with an
expectation that auditors will work through many
organisational processes in any one day as well as provide
accurate reports within specific timeframes to the
certification agency and organisation. If you prefer to take
your time to perform tasks or make decisions, then you
might need to think about how to manage the volume of
work in a different way than in the past.

➤ Review your approach to receiving feedback, including
from clients, work colleagues and team members as well
as from mentors. Feedback is an important aspect of this
work and helps you to grow and refine your knowledge as
an auditor.

➤ Actively know your capabilities to lead as well as to
follow. Auditors frequently change roles from one
audit to the next. People who prefer to lead and not
follow – and vice versa – can find being on an audit
team comprising of a number of other auditors to be
a challenging experience. If you are used to being 'the

boss' and directing people to perform certain tasks regardless of how they feel about that, or if you feel more comfortable to have other people take on the leadership role, there may be some challenging consequences if you don't reconsider your approach. There are some situations where you will be the sole auditor and there are other situations where you will be part of a team of people undertaking an audit in a particular timeframe.

> Never underestimate the skills associated with being a valued and productive team member! There is nothing worse that working on a team with an auditor who withholds information from other team members or perhaps has an ego about being the Lead Auditor. Similarly, challenges arise when the Lead Auditor does not have the capacity to manage sometimes difficult conversations with organisations or to address serious matters within the audit context. Being aware of your strengths and weaknesses in these areas is critical to being a successful auditor.

> Search websites for prospective certification bodies and firms that employ or engage contracted auditors. Online networking can assist in your search, as can contacts amongst networks and discussions with people who know of reputable certification firms. The goal of these searches is to find a certification body that is closely aligned to your own values and abilities. While new auditors may initially be concerned about the amounts of money they may make as a Lead Auditor, it is important to feel comfortable with the certification body as you could be doing a lot of work with people you rarely see. It is important to trust and have access to these people when you need guidance.

What to expect once you start

Along with completing the required Lead Auditor training, taking the time to investigate and consider these factors can assist you to be more fully prepared for what to expect. The organisation or certification body you choose to work with will also have their own guidelines and processes for building your knowledge. These processes generally include completing an initial orientation program with the certification agency and then progressing through observations and support auditor functions with an audit team.

Graded stepping through audit team roles

Once you have completed the Lead Auditor training and the certification body's internal orientation program, you will be engaged as a Novice or Observer Auditor in the first instance. In this role, you will assume the role of an observer, which generally involves watching the audit process and not actively contributing towards the audit itself. You may be expected to observe a number of audits until you feel confident to progress onto the second step, which involves the more active responsibilities associated with being a Support Auditor.

Before your first experience as a Novice, take the time to study the standards and read a bit about the service to be audited so you have some information about what the audit will be covering. You may feel unsure about what to expect – this is normal. Generally, the Lead Auditor will be in contact with you before the first audit to answer any questions you may have, to provide reassurance, as well as to address practicalities such as where the organisation is located, parking and where to meet before entering the building.

Learn from your Lead Auditor

Take the valuable opportunity to learn from your Lead Auditor. The Lead Auditor on my first audit was actively seeking evidence to confirm how the organisation met the standards, while also being mindful of the fact that I was attending as the Novice Auditor. From the opening meeting with the organisation's CEO and her staff, the Lead Auditor checked in with me to see how well I understood the process and the tools I would be expected to use in subsequent audits.

The Lead Auditor provided a range of valued supports to me, along with the opportunity to understand the mechanics of the audit process in a safe environment. I was not expected to comment or actively contribute towards what he was doing. Instead, I was given time to listen and observe the audit tasks and to learn how the audit tools worked in practice.

What I observed of the actions taken by the Lead Auditor during the audit quickly demonstrated to me the need to think rapidly while at the same time being focused on what was happening in the moment. For example, when interviewing board members, staff or clients I realised that additional insights could be gleaned from watching body language and the ways people interact with one another. Even the flick of an eyebrow could be telling! I also realised that the ability to recall details that I might have seen or heard earlier in the day for something that was happening later that same day or perhaps the next day in another context were critical skills to have as well.

What to expect

Observing the audit process will show you how the Lead Auditor and other members of an audit team communicate with one another and the organisation. You will also see how they encourage, guide, support, review, direct and sometimes educate the people working for the organisation through a fast-paced day.

Regardless of how busy the day is, it is important you have the opportunity to ask questions and to understand how the process works. I can recall feeling unsure about what I needed to do during my first audit, and I have often seen Novice Auditors experiencing similar uncertainty about what the day will hold and what I will provide in the way of support.

At the end of the first day, I have seen Novice or Observer Auditors walk away from the audit either feeling equipped for the next phase of their development or feeling like they need to reconsider what they expect of a usual audit work schedule. For example, some Novice or Observer Auditors feel overwhelmed about how much has to be covered in one day and some people say they had not expected the pace to be quite so busy. Yet other Novice or Observer Auditors easily step into the pace and requirements. It is a very individual response! Some people undertake a number of observation audits before progressing any further, while other people move quickly to the Support Auditor role.

Some people choose to remain a Support Auditor for the duration of their auditing career. Others find they need more assistance to understand the professional nature of their role. Some Support Auditors assume technical expert roles which complement the Lead Auditor's work.

There are many ways that auditors can progress. It is important that you speak up about whether you are ready to take on further roles, or whether you need a bit more time. Personally, I was able to step into the Support Auditor role quite quickly and I appreciated the ongoing support of the Lead Auditor as I developed confidence about the audit process and its requirements. I often worried about saying the wrong thing, leaving out essential information or getting the steps mixed up. I soon came to appreciate that every auditor goes through these concerns!

When you don't immediately understand everything ...

As far as I am concerned, there is no such thing as a silly question! The truth is that all auditors, regardless of level, have to start somewhere. It is essential that you understand you are learning new skills and abilities and you won't know everything to begin with.

There is a lot to understand, not only related to the different requirements of each standard, but also to meet the specific requirements of the certification body. Managing yourself professionally when working with clients is critically important – and you will find yourself in many different situations where people passively or actively resist the audit process, or just want it over and done with to get the certification, regardless of the way you have approached the audit. However, the audits where people genuinely welcome and appreciate what you have contributed provide so many opportunities to strengthen and reinforce the influence and impact you can make, as well as confirm to the organisation what an incredibly valuable resource an audit can be.

Reflections

How did you know that your skills and abilities would be a good match with what is required to be an auditor?

....

....

....

....

Looking at the list of suggestions earlier in this chapter, did you do all of these before you started – or none at all?

....

....

....

....

If you have completed observation audits, were there any actions taken by the Lead Auditor that surprised you?

....

....

....

....

....

Progressing from Novice Auditor to Support Auditor can take some time. Have you thought about how long it could take you and how you will manage this?

....

....

....

....

What aspects of auditing would you like to know more about now? Who do you think you can ask?

....

....

....

....

....

....

....

....

....

3.

LEVELS OF AUDITOR

Greatness is not a function of circumstance. Greatness, it turns out, is largely a matter of conscious choice and discipline.

(JIM COLLINS)

Auditor levels

What I have seen over the years is that auditors need to have a defined portfolio of skills, knowledge and abilities that support their professional audit approach. People frequently come into the role with a lot of previous experience that they can use in a practical way in the audits they manage.

In the following table you can see there are a number of auditor levels. Each level has a specific function, role and focus, and delivers a different result. From what I have seen, the different auditor levels also provide varying value to the organisations and businesses they audit, ranging from little tangible value through to significant influencing capabilities.

LEVELS	TYPE	FOCUS	POSITION	RESULT	VALUE
LEVEL 5	AMBASSADOR	LEVERAGE	INFLUENCER	STRENGTH	+90%+
LEVEL 4	EXPERT	INSIGHT	PRODUCER	VALUE	+70%
LEVEL 3	LEAD	COMPLIANCE	GUIDE	ASSURANCE	+40%
LEVEL 2	SUPPORT	COMPETENCE	CONTRIBUTOR	ASSISTANCE	-10%
LEVEL 1	NOVICE	SYSTEM	FOLLOWER	INVISIBLE	-20%

Level 1: *Novice or Observer Auditor*

People commencing their journey as an auditor will have completed a Lead Auditor course or other relevant quality management qualifications. However, in order to address the expectations of certification bodies, they are required to understand the practical and professional aspects of auditing through onsite observations. They are not expected to actively contribute towards the audit tasks or process. Instead, they observe the tasks that are being undertaken and have the opportunity to learn about the tools and techniques being implemented within an auditing process.

Generally, the Lead Auditor who has the overall responsibility for the audit will check in from time to time to monitor how the novice is progressing, and there are usually many opportunities for the Novice Auditor to ask questions.

Occasionally, the Novice Auditor may also observe other auditors on an auditing team. This enables the Novice Auditor to extend their knowledge and capacity through observing the ways different auditors manage the audit process.

Novice Auditors may take some time to develop their competence and confidence, or they may quite quickly step into the role of the Support Auditor and refine their understanding and knowledge of the audit process.

Level 2: *Support Auditor*

The Support Auditor is guided by the Lead Auditor to implement and conduct some of the audit tasks identified on the audit plan. Support Auditors often work on tasks independently, but regularly check in with the Lead Auditor. In some cases, and depending on their existing skill level, the Support Auditor may have some responsibility for interviewing stakeholders and for analysing the data and documentary detail they are reviewing. Some people choose to remain a Support Auditor, preferring not to undertake the training required to become a Lead Auditor or to take on the responsibilities associated with managing and conducting audits.

Support Auditors generally have specific and practical experience that adds some value to the overall audit plan and process. Their contributions assist the Lead Auditor to complete the requirements of the audit in a timely manner. It is important for Support Auditors to realise that they have the right to explain their decisions during the audit. Support Auditors are *not* less important than the Lead Auditor: they are auditors who are developing and refining their skills and confidence. Occasionally, Support Auditors tell me they are afraid to challenge the Lead Auditor's decisions or actions, particularly if these are considered to be unprofessional, ill-considered or one-sided. Support Auditors should always speak up in these situations. Power imbalances should be resolved as soon as possible.

Level 3: *Lead Auditor*

A Lead Auditor has completed a Lead Auditor course or relevant quality management training as well as the mandatory requirements associated with completing the certification body's internal auditor practice obligations.

Lead Auditors focus on the tasks identified in the audit plan as well as continually referring to the compliance requirements identified in the standards and program guidelines applicable to the service provider's business. Depending on the Lead Auditor's experience and approach, they may conduct either a straightforward, checklist approach to the audit or they might add insights based on their own professional background and experience.

However, Lead Auditors who are proficient and competent in managing the tasks associated with conducting an audit are well placed to provide assurance of what must be done to ensure the standards are met. They often guide the organisation through compliance-related practices, providing some relevant information to assist the process.

Level 4: *Expert Auditor*

Lead Auditors with extensive industry or sector experience are known as Expert Auditors. They may also be well known in the sector or industry. Organisations often feel very reassured when an Expert Auditor with an innate understanding about the nuances of their sector conducts their audit.

Frequently, auditors at this level provide valued insights into the standards and how they affect the organisation's business operations. They often provide multi-layered and practical information that can help the organisation minimise unnecessary risk.

Expert Auditors often seek to understand the 'why' underpinning the organisation's strategies and tasks and can appreciate the context of the actions taken to address the standards and indicators. Auditors with this mindset frequently discover examples about how people actively work towards the organisation's mission and purpose, what gets done and why, how activities have been improved and refined over time, and the difference these tasks make in the lives of clients.

This is an approach that considers performance and outcomes rather than solely relying on policies and procedures to gauge an organisation's progress in meeting the standards.

Level 5: *Ambassador Auditor*

An Ambassador Auditor takes their expertise further into the realm of influence, inspiration and impact. They have the knack for seeing the entire organisational context while also being aware of the operational practices that are required to meet nominated goals, long-term vision and strategic purpose. They have the ability to assess the challenges organisations face, while also having access to their own stores of knowledge to assist the organisation to strengthen their strategic practices. Their knowledge encourages and, in fact, calls upon CEOs and their organisations to step up and demonstrate best practice – not only with governance practices, but also with focused attention on the internal and external clients as well as on strategies that strengthen the service provider and its business activities.

Ambassador Auditors frequently employ courageous communication techniques to explore and, where possible, expose 'blind spots' that could be detrimental to the organisation's progress. They are comfortable in being able to go beyond what may be viewed as safe practices within an audit process. Using their wealth of knowledge, experience and commitment, they readily identify and name the areas which may present issues to the business as well as identifying areas that could be strengthened and enhanced.

Through their continued search for knowledge and insight into organisational excellence, Ambassador Auditors become known for their commitment towards strengthening not only the organisations being audited but also for making improvements to sector and industry practice. They share their knowledge with other people and often have the capacity and willingness to influence industry leaders, including through challenging deep-seated, perhaps unstated, beliefs and raising the expectation for professional practice.

However, this is not solely an outward-focused approach: Ambassador Auditors rigorously challenge their *own* blind spots and beliefs as well. Sometimes Ambassador Auditors work with mentors to examine these deep-seated practices and at other times they contribute towards the mentor's own professional practice.

While some auditors become Ambassador Auditors without even realising this is the level they are operating at, other auditors acknowledge the effort put into mastering their own skills and knowledge. In some cases, Ambassador Auditors may be humble yet incredibly effective in their abilities. Most often, they shun pomposity and showmanship. However, they have a long-term view and are fully aware of their purpose in strengthening not only what the sector and industry can achieve over a long period of time, but also what improvements can be made for the world at large.

Reflections

Considering the various auditor levels. What level do you think you are?

....

....

....

....

Were you aware that there were levels beyond being a Lead Auditor? How does this knowledge influence your auditing profile?

....

....

....

....

What value do you see yourself bringing to an organisation that you are auditing? Could you contribute more?

....

....

....

....

Is the value you believe you bring to an audit aligned with a particular auditor level explained in this chapter? If not, what can you do about that?

....

....

....

....

From your own experiences, how do the auditors you know or work alongside consider their level? Do you think they consider the value resulting from the audits they conduct?

....

....

....

....

....

....

....

....

....

4.

DIFFERENT AUDITOR STYLES

Open the window of your mind.
Allow the fresh air, new lights
and new truths to enter.

(AMIT RAY)

Auditors frequently have different styles and approaches to their work, and this is often apparent early in their auditing career. When they start out, many auditors tend to operate from a purely compliance-focused position, which means they tend to view the standards as a range of work tasks and 'to-do' practices and expect the organisation to be doing exactly what the standards and indicators say.

Auditors with a compliance-only mindset

Auditors operating with a compliance mindset might use techniques drawing on the fear of 'being caught doing the wrong thing' as the incentive for the organisation to comply with the required standards and indicators. In this situation, the auditor is generally searching for evidence that demonstrates compliance and, as a result, may be viewed by the organisation as being pedantic or bureaucratic in their search for gaps and non-conformities. The auditor may make few allowances for nuances or the context the organisation is operating within, and even less for acknowledging innovation, how people problem-solve in complex environments or how ideas are shared to make improvements to the business operations. Outcomes for clients may not be considered at all, since the auditor's focus primarily remains on verifying that the standards are being met.

As the Novice Auditor progresses into the Support Auditor role, they might continue to operate in this compliance-focused manner. This can occur when the auditor does not question the need to audit in a less rigid way, given the focus on the need to comply with set requirements built into various standards as well as the focus on compliance that is taught in the Lead Auditor training courses. For many auditors, compliance-focused auditing can appear to be more clear-cut, with the result that findings and decisions may be easier to explain. The truth is that compliance-focused auditing can feel safe in many ways. However, solely operating with this type of approach can have negative as well as positive outcomes for organisations.

The impact of compliance-only thinking on organisations

Compliance audits tend to make a black-and-white comparison with a set of standards and take people down the path of least complexity. Such an approach tends to reinforce the organisation's comfort zone and to provide evidence that demonstrates compliance to the bare minimum of the relevant standards.

Organisations that are audited using a compliance-only mindset may consider this to be a positive outcome when they only want to achieve certification and are not interested in ways to strengthen their practices. Compliance-focused auditors can frequently address the organisation's requirements without needing to draw upon additional skills or knowledge.

When this type of auditor uses a checklist approach, the outcome might result in references to policies, procedures, a range of registers, forms, databases, staff and client protocols, governance practices, and examples of reports and information provided to relevant stakeholders. It can appear to be a case of 'You have a policy on XYZ: tick. That complies with the standard.' However, checklists don't explain *how* any of these procedures work in practice or *what* they mean in assisting the organisation to achieve its purpose. In effect, checklists often only confirm that the organisation has these processes in place – or does not have them in place, as the case may be.

When auditors focus solely on compliance when an organisation is seeking additional insights and value-added detail, the organisation can be left feeling as if they have not acquired anything extra compared to what they could have done themselves using a checklist.

Focusing on compliance to the exclusion of factors related to organisational growth and profitability within today's dynamic organisational environment is not enough for many organisations and businesses. Researchers have found that this sort of audit approach can be a deterrent to progress and impede organisational growth and innovation.

However, while these audits continue to be perceived as

'police enforcement with little or no visible added value', the reality is that auditing is not meant to catch people out or be fault-finding missions. Instead, auditing is meant to highlight and demonstrate that the organisation's systems are working as they are meant to, and ideally also result in insights that can be used by the organisation to make improvements to their systems over time.

For organisations that want more from the audit process, auditors will be expected to draw on a number of skills and knowledge related to assessing, reviewing and evaluating systems, processes, services and outcomes as well as an understanding and appreciation of the way the organisation interacts with its internal and external stakeholders. In these cases, the focus may be less on reviewing records and documents and more on other processes that demonstrate how the organisation is addressing the *intent* of the standards and indicators.

I have found that there are many opportunities for auditors to hold a mirror to processes and organisations. The ability to provide valuable feedback and recommendations that address areas for continual improvement and innovation is often appreciated. This is where the auditor's professional experience, sensibility and expertise can add a great deal of value to organisations and areas being reviewed.

What is expected

As auditors step further into their role, there are many opportunities for personal and professional growth. While this approach comes back to the auditor and what they want to achieve from their auditing role, there are many external pressures on auditors to provide a high standard with the audit process. Organisations are expecting more as well.

From what I have seen of auditors who make a difference to organisations and the broader sector with their work, the following factors are often apparent:

> **READINESS** – to step up and offer more
> **OPENNESS** – to learning from feedback and continued professional development
> **COMMITMENT** – to being the best possible auditor
> **KNOWLEDGE** – not just of the standards, but also of broader best practice in business principles
> **MASTERY** – of techniques and of personal practice
> **INFLUENCE** – strength of character based on solid, thought-leader experience
> **IMPACT** – making a real difference for the client organisation and the broader community as well as for the profession of auditing.

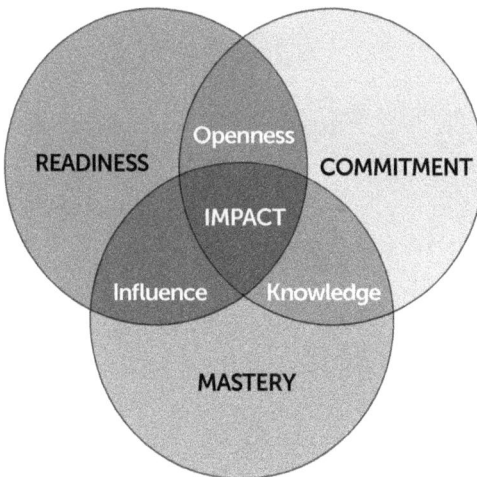

Regardless of how people come to their role as an auditor, one thing is certain: it is a profession that is not for the faint-hearted! Today's businesses and organisations generally require the auditor and auditing team to provide more than a checklist response. This means auditors need to keep abreast of business management practices, not only in their particular sector, but across a wide array of sources.

In many instances, auditors are catalysts for change, providing an opportunity to stimulate and encourage organisations to go beyond what the standards say. Having additional information and insights gleaned from continual learning avenues can add value in ways organisations may not have noticed for themselves.

You can choose courage, or you can choose comfort, but you cannot choose both.
(BRENÉ BROWN)

Reflections

What do you expect to offer in your role as an auditor? Do you see yourself offering more than a compliance audit?

....

....

....

....

Have you witnessed a compliance-only mindset being used for an audit process? What were the effects of this?

....

....

....

....

What would you do if you were part of a compliance-focus audit approach when it seemed that the organisation might expect more from the audit?

....

....

....

....

How do you keep abreast of current, best practice business methods? Are you a member of business or professional organisations that focus on best practice and the sharing of knowledge?

....

....

....

....

....

....

Do you subscribe to journals or conduct your own research about business management topics? What benefits might you expect from continually reviewing a broader knowledge base?

....

....

....

....

....

....

....

5.

WHAT MAKES A GOOD AUDITOR

A leader is one who knows the way,
goes the way and shows the way.
(JOHN C MAXWELL)

Auditor attributes and qualities

Considerable research has been conducted during the past twenty years about the different attributes an auditor brings to an audit as well as the satisfaction levels experienced by organisations and businesses with the audit process. The following table summarises some opinions about the required attributes and qualities of successful auditors.

SOURCE	DESIRED AUDITOR ATTRIBUTES AND QUALITIES
Bonner & Pennington[2]	The ability to: ➤ retrieve knowledge from experience and industry as well as social and financial factors – plus continue to search for relevant external information ➤ maintain broad and relevant business management knowledge ➤ verify evidence and information rapidly and accurately ➤ deliver high levels of comprehension and accuracy ➤ generate plausible hypotheses ➤ develop normative judgement responses ➤ maintain high levels of consensus with the team and the client.
American Society for Quality[3]	The ability to be: ➤ independent ➤ systematic ➤ trustworthy ➤ persistent ➤ positive ➤ curious ➤ open-minded ➤ mature ➤ tenacious ➤ patient ➤ adaptable ➤ unbiased ➤ courageous ➤ ethical ➤ diplomatic ➤ versatile ➤ without a hidden agenda.

SOURCE	DESIRED AUDITOR ATTRIBUTES AND QUALITIES	
International Standards Organisation (ISO 9001)[4]	The ability to be: › ethical › diplomatic › observant › perceptive › versatile › tenacious › decisive › self-reliant › open to improvement › culturally sensitive	› collaborative › able to act with fortitude.
Forbes[5]	The ability to: › use technology › use relevant communication skills › think critically and use relevant investigative skills › work across silos to provide a more complete picture of the organisation › look ahead and have a 'forward view' (e.g. not just focus on the current types of technology but consider future options) › 'mine' data for information that is important to clients (e.g. issues affecting relevant risks, internal controls, important processes) › provide ideas for making the organisation more efficient and enhancing internal controls.	

SOURCE	DESIRED AUDITOR ATTRIBUTES AND QUALITIES
Anderson[6]	The ability to: ‣ use instincts ‣ see the big picture and the vision for the organisation ‣ use relevant people skills in a range of situations ‣ use relevant decision-making skills ‣ maintain personal and professional leadership skills ‣ use superior communication skills.
Wahid, Grigg & Prajogo[7]	The ability to be: ‣ ethical and professional ‣ objective ‣ articulate, confident, pleasant and diplomatic ‣ flexible and adaptive ‣ able to use good judgement ‣ fair and open-minded ‣ a good listener ‣ a good time-keeper ‣ a problem solver ‣ observant and perceptive ‣ positive in attitude and approach ‣ reliable and operating from a place of integrity.

Forbes Insights and KPMG[8] also conducted research into desired auditor skills, which include:

1. Having a demonstrated professional approach to the audit process.
2. Having recognised and desirable experience in the organisation's industry.
3. Effective investigative skills.
4. Effective team management practices.
5. Operating more like a partner and providing insights to enable the business to become more effective and, in some cases, to operate more competitively.
6. Providing specific observations and recommendations that can add value, not just a 'laundry list of ideas', and to 'take things to the next level' through actionable information for the organisation.
7. Having more business and governance skills and abilities than those within the organisation may have themselves.
8. Having an amplified focus on the forward-trending of risks and insights that lead to proactive quality assurance and regulatory compliance.
9. Providing a deeper analysis within the audit process.
10. Being a critical thinker and able to rapidly analyse data, documents and situations.
11. Continually improving interpersonal communication and people skills.
12. Having effective conflict resolution skills.
13. Developing effective and professionally written audit reports.
14. Understanding the implications of rapidly changing technology.

Continuity is also seen in a positive light, particularly when the auditor develops a deep understanding of the organisation's business, and what is important and not important, as well as being aware of how the organisation's business is different from other businesses, services and organisations in their industry.

While some CEOs do not want any more from the audit than to obtain a certificate stating the organisation complies with the required standards, other CEOs actively seek specific insights to strengthen their operations. In some cases, CEOs state they do not want audit results to be the same as for the previous year, nor do they want a compliance verification that is viewed as 'police enforcement with no or little visible added value'.[9] CEOs are increasingly demanding a higher level of attention within an audit as well as an amplified focus on the forward-trending of risks and insights that lead to proactive quality assurance and regulatory compliance.

For organisations operating in a competitive market environment, the days when an audit focused solely on compliance appear to be a relic of the past.

Deploying good attributes

LEVELS	TYPE	FOCUS	POSITION	RESULT	VALUE
LEVEL 5	AMBASSADOR	LEVERAGE	INFLUENCER	STRENGTH	+ 90% +
LEVEL 4	EXPERT	INSIGHT	PRODUCER	VALUE	+ 70%
LEVEL 3	LEAD	COMPLIANCE	GUIDE	ASSURANCE	+ 40%
LEVEL 2	SUPPORT	COMPETENCE	CONTRIBUTOR	ASSISTANCE	-10%
LEVEL 1	NOVICE	SYSTEM	FOLLOWER	INVISIBLE	-20%

As we progress into the 2020s, organisations and businesses are moving further into the world of standards and compliance at a time when they are exposed to increased competition, the impact of advances in technology as well as the pressure to engage staff who can perform increasingly more sophisticated tasks and responsibilities. At the same time, expectations about the quality and value of the auditor's approach towards the organisation or business continue to increase.

Regardless of your auditing role, you will be expected to provide increasingly high standards of performance and integrity in each and every interaction you have with all levels of staff, board members and stakeholders as well as clients.

For people progressing from Novice to Support Auditor and onwards to a Lead Auditor position, developing and working with a range of skills and abilities that complement the initial Lead Auditor training as well as the certification body's on-boarding program will be required. In many ways, you will continue to incorporate a checklist process to audit and assess the organisation's practices and operations against particular standards until you develop confidence with the audit requirements.

Attributes of a Lead Auditor

As you step more fully into the Lead Auditor role, you will assume different responsibilities, not least of which include working with different teams and being responsible for the team's behaviour while focusing on the tasks identified in the audit plan and meeting nominated deadlines.

An effective Lead Auditor cares for and supports the team before, during and after the audit, making sure that the fundamentals such as accommodation, nourishment, transport as well as the components they will be undertaking during the audit are managed. Checking in during the audit can provide the team with the opportunity to share concerns and issues as well as identify the organisation's strengths. Checking in also provides valuable time to debrief, when needed, after challenging interviews. An effective Lead Auditor also checks in after the audit has finished to see if there was anything extra that could have been provided or done differently.

As the Lead Auditor, you will be expected to rapidly yet accurately sort out connections and linkages within the organisation in order to focus the audit approach for the duration of the audit. You will develop further understanding about the requirements of the standards and use your previous experience in the areas you audit to clearly convey thoughts, ideas and suggestions in meetings with board members, staff and clients as well as in presentations, negotiations and interviews.

The days when auditors could say, '*You are expected to comply with the standards and that is the end of the story*' are long gone. Today's organisations expect a lot more from an audit or assessment process than that.

Being an effective and capable Lead Auditor

But what exactly is an effective and capable Lead Auditor? What skills, attributes and qualities does a successful Lead Auditor need? In the Forbes and KPMG research, the results highlighted the importance of the auditor's communication skills, along with their ability to articulate a clear point of view on the issues affecting clients as well as the organisation or business.[10] These skills may involve the use of effective and respectful conflict management techniques during difficult conversations, which can happen at any time during an audit or assessment.

Of course, the ability to listen – with your ears, heart and mind – is critically important. Active listening helps the Lead Auditor to understand and comprehend what is being explained or demonstrated. Sometimes a lot of listening is required before the Lead Auditor can make any explanations.

Effective communication skills are definitely required when guiding and, in some ways, educating people about nuances in standards as well as when assisting organisations through audits. Again, the ability to listen and comprehend as you are guiding people through the process can elicit deeper levels of information and provide the organisation with a stronger method for being understood. As Stephen Covey so ably states, '*Listen with the intent to understand, not the intent to reply.*'[11]

In your Lead Auditor role, you will find that today's audits and assessments frequently go beyond the realms of a 'tick-box' exercise, with many opportunities to bring people along on a journey of discovery about what the standards can mean for the organisation or business.

The role of emotional intelligence

In many ways, your IQ is only part of being an effective and capable Lead Auditor: emotional intelligence[12] (also known as EQ) is also needed. This means you must excel at maintaining your composure during sometimes challenging and difficult conversations, particularly where the CEO or board may not agree with the decisions you are making about a particular standard. Your ability to ask intelligent yet respectful questions and make suggestions that demonstrate your awareness of the context and issues confronting the organisation can enhance the overall audit process, particularly when you bring in your own experience around matters affecting the organisation.

Genuine empathy and active listening skills are critically important, as organisations grapple with challenging business decisions and functions on a daily basis. When you use these skills, you demonstrate your understanding and comprehension of specific issues for the organisation, ones that may be very different to other audit experiences.

Respect is crucial, as is compassion and the ability to walk with people through a process that they may not relish or want. These approaches enhance the auditor's credibility and go a long way towards building trust for the organisation. Without trust, audits are incredibly difficult to navigate.

During any part of the audit, you might feel calm and operate with a level head in your Lead Auditor role, but the staff, CEO and board members of the organisation may not be operating in the same way. They may be frustrated and disappointed about the things you are finding, and they may be wondering how they are going to resolve the issues you have identified.

Sometimes people are already exhausted before you have arrived, not only in preparing for the audit but in managing the day-to-day operations of the business. I recall one situation where the CEO had been awake for almost twenty-four hours straight when I arrived onsite to start a three-day recertification assessment. There had been an emergency in one of the accommodation houses managed by the organisation and industrial action had been taken during that time. As a result, staff had walked off the job during the previous 12 hours, leaving a cleaner and one support person to assist and care for several clients with high-support needs. Flooding in the local community had effectively prevented other staff from being able to access the house and, as a result, the CEO had stepped in to provide back-up assistance while sourcing relief staff from a large staffing agency located nearby.

When I arrived, the CEO was in the latter stage of engaging external staff to cover the emergency situation and looked completely exhausted. One look at this man and I could see that he wasn't prepared to engage in an audit and a momentary flash of annoyance in his eyes showed me that he was pretty irritated about me being in the reception area. I could see he was incredibly stressed and that his personal exhaustion levels were having a toll on his ability to maintain his usual strong self-control. I rapidly decided that an opening meeting would be ridiculous in this situation and instead made him a coffee and toast while he worked out the next steps with his administration staff to address the situation. I really felt for him: having these sorts of situations occur at any time is tough enough, let alone having these happen when an auditor arrives.

After making a joke about him having to deal with the last person any organisation wants to see (me), in a matter of minutes we had worked out a plan for the day so he knew what I would be doing in amongst the work he would be doing to address the clients' needs. I assured him I was more than able to work with the changed circumstances, and when we caught up the next day, he said my calm approach had enabled him to focus on what was important at the time.

Events like this happen in audits and it is the ability to provide genuine assurances that can really make a difference for everyone. Research has found that the use of emotional intelligence can improve audit quality, particularly through the moderation of different pressures on the auditor's judgements at the time.[13] It certainly would not have helped the situation for the CEO if I had lost my composure, become annoyed, looked completely rattled by his approach or expected to simply get on with the audit, regardless of what was happening!

The role of critical thinking

Effective Lead Auditors need to provide assurances to the organisation about where and how they meet – or don't meet – the required standards. Critical thinking assists in the objective analysis and evaluation of the information provided by the organisation or business and provides the basis for producing actionable insights that the organisation can use once the audit has finished. In some cases, critical thinking provides an opportunity for the auditor or assessor to ask questions that the organisation may not have considered before and can lead to further discussion and questions that may inspire the organisation.

Curiosity is a strength in an audit, providing the opportunity to view problems in a positive way and to seek answers to potential mysteries. Many Lead Auditors find that when they return to the organisation for the next audit, staff express delight in the opportunity to share what they have done following the auditor's questions and, in some cases, may have taken action beyond what was originally envisaged.

Using critical thinking to inform key questions frequently demonstrates the Lead Auditor's understanding of the organisation and the sector in which it operates. Having a wide range of business knowledge and experience also assists the auditor to critically think about what the standards mean for the organisation and to 'connect the dots' when reviewing evidence during the audit. Sometimes Lead Auditors use critical thinking and subsequent questioning in a prescriptive manner to enable the organisation to clearly understand where the required improvements should be made.

There is a risk, however, when the Lead Auditor becomes fixated on one or two particular issues to the exclusion of the organisation's overall approach to address the requirements of the standards. Moreover, slowly working through the specific details stated in a particular standard without viewing the organisation as a whole can slow the momentum down.

In his well-known book *The E-Myth Revisited*, Michael Gerber talks about working 'on' the business, instead of solely focusing 'in' the business, with references to the fatal assumption that an individual who understands the technical work of a business can successfully run a business that does the technical work.[14] When considering the role of the Lead Auditor, it can feel like you take both an overarching view of the organisation and what it does, while also diving into particular strategies and practices that inform the achievement of the organisation's goals and vision.

The reality is that an effective and capable Lead Auditor needs to have both capabilities: the overarching view of the organisation's 'big picture' as well as an awareness of the detail that makes the organisation work on a daily basis. As an effective Lead Auditor, you have to have an eye on both facets, and also have the courage and strength of character to re-examine evidence if something seems to be incomplete or does not 'add up' when reviewing how both the 'big picture' and the daily operations intersect and work in practice.

Exuding professional and executive presence frequently facilitates and inspires confidence and trust from people at all organisational levels, particularly when difficult details need to be shared and discussed. Being transparent in your approach throughout the audit also encourages people to feel confident about your integrity, credibility and authenticity during both the straightforward and challenging conversations you will have with many different stakeholders.

However, not all Lead Auditors have these higher order qualities and skills or appreciate how these could contribute to making them competent and effective in their role. It all comes back to your own approach, of course, and how you view the Lead Auditor role. The skills, abilities and qualities required by effective Lead Auditors require commitment and ongoing dedicated effort in order to continuously strengthen and refine their practice.

Reflections

As you can see, a lot of research has been conducted into desired auditor qualities and attributes. How many of these qualities and attributes do you consider you have?

....

....

....

....

What will you do if you realise there are critical attributes or qualities that you don't have?

....

....

....

....

Who do you trust to tell you the truth and give you honest feedback about your qualities and attributes?

....

....

....

....

If you feel that your EQ skills need improving, who would you ask to help you?

....

....

....

....

Do you believe you exude executive presence? How do you demonstrate this?

....

....

....

....

....

....

....

....

....

....

....

6.

WHAT AUDITORS REALLY DO

The ultimate measure of a man is not where he stands in moments of comfort and convenience, but where he stands at times of challenge and controversy.
(MARTIN LUTHER KING JR)

As we enter the 2020s, the process through which an audit or assessment is undertaken continues to challenge the robustness of the internal controls and processes an organisation has in place, giving an external perspective and the provision of valuable feedback. This means the focus of audits and assessments is taking a stronger role in future-proofing organisations and providing assurances of trust, integrity and transparency of management and service delivery practices to clients.

Effective audits and assessments often provide organisations with crucial information about the validity of their operational practices, possible or actual weaknesses or risk, opportunities for improvement, identification of fraud or unethical practices, and areas where the business or organisation is effective and operating according to its purpose.

At the same time, it is critically important to remember than any audit is conducted at a particular point in time, which means that what you see today may be different to what will be seen tomorrow. There may also be subtle differences, based on who is looking at the evidence and what their particular framework and professional experience has been. Similarly, we have to be mindful of the fact that the organisation or business being audited is a complex and dynamic system that is not standing still.[15]

This means that auditors need to look at the interactions and relationships between a system's components as they are shaped and affected by the system itself. This goes well beyond the standard compliance check or cause-and-effect review, and requires the auditor to study and review, at the very least, the relationships between practices, documentation and outcomes.

Reviewing the links between these processes can provide much-appreciated insight – or an experience of frustration and downright annoyance. A lot depends on the interactions between the auditor and the organisation, as well as who else is involved and what is being assessed. But what, exactly, do auditors do?

Tasks to be completed in an audit

Simply put, an auditor conducts interviews, observes processes, examines and reviews documents and records, and then assesses and evaluates how effectively an organisation's systems meet its own requirements as well as those identified in particular standards. This involves the auditor analysing the processes used by an organisation and comparing what is undertaken on a daily basis with how it is managed with the stated procedures, work instructions and standards before establishing the gaps. By interviewing different stakeholders as well as clients, along with reviewing a range of documents, there are many opportunities for obtaining insights into how effectively these practices are operating. Auditors work to ascertain that what an organisation does in fact do what it says it does, then meets the pertinent standards, legislative and regulatory requirements. This approach is extended to confirm that what happens in practice also meets the purpose, objectives and outcomes identified in the organisation's overall vision and mission statements. As part of this review, the auditor prepares a report that objectively analyses not only what was sighted as evidence in the audit, but also assesses the audit outcome against the standards being evaluated and the experience of clients and other stakeholders. Auditors often incorporate considerations about best practice for the sector or industry into this analysis.

Auditor responsibilities

Auditors have many responsibilities. These frequently involve:

> - Project managing the audit (e.g. developing the audit plan; engaging with other members of the audit team to address specific audit plan requirements and where each member will be working; managing travel and accommodation arrangements; making preliminary contact with the organisation before the onsite or desktop audit).
> - Professionally conducting the audit:
>   - against an agreed set of standards

- through the review of evidence that demonstrates
   compliance with the agreed standard
- through the assessment of risk and determining how
   risk mitigation practices operate for the organisation
- in a confidential and respectful manner
- by assessing the controls for compliance and adequacy.

> When necessary, assisting the organisation to understand the meaning and interpretations of the standards.

> Ensuring the organisation is kept aware of the progress of the audit or assessment process.

> Ensuring reports are professionally prepared and completed within the specific timeframes. This involves checking sentence structure and spelling as well as accuracy, clarity and flow of logic and findings before sending the reports through to the organisation.

> Addressing any unforeseen or complicating factors after the audit or assessment has been completed.

> Providing advice to funding bodies and/or the certification body about the audit process, when needed.

> Maintaining professional qualifications and membership of professional associations in quality auditing.

Additional auditor practices

Effective auditors go beyond the use of a template checklist linked to the standards and indicators, and generally don't have preconceived ideas about how the audit will unfold before arriving onsite or conducting the audit remotely from the organisation's location. Having an open mind and a curious approach can assist the auditor to delve more deeply into the actual practices of the organisation and to develop a deeper appreciation for what the organisation is attempting to achieve over time.

The word 'auditor' is derived from the Latin word for 'listener' or 'hearer', and the ability to hear and listen with different senses can really assist an auditor to see more of what is happening than what a written procedure can reveal.

Through the auditor's use of simple yet applicable open-ended questions, opportunities are provided for people to respond to far more than what the indicator statements in the standards say. Sometimes the responses provide time for reflection and an acknowledgement of what is being done well. At other times, the responses highlight people's awareness that what the policies or procedures say isn't what is actually done in practice.

Auditor self-awareness

Without having some appreciation of the impact of our words or actions, other people's lives can be changed in ways we could never imagine. It is easy to get wrapped up in our own world and not consider what we bring into audit situations and, by extension, the lives of other people. Having some semblance of personal awareness or an appreciation for the fact that our personal beliefs and biases can affect situations and others are important considerations for auditors – regardless of whether they are aware of taking on the role of change agent or not.

It is also important to be aware that our conscious and unconscious behaviour, words, actions and body language provides information to clients and the people working for the organisations and businesses we are auditing. Similarly, we often make our internal judgements about situations based on how people or situations are presented to us. Effective auditors are aware of these factors and monitor their approach throughout the entire audit process to ensure there is no disconnect between what is intended and not intended, particularly with building and maintaining trustworthiness.

The following diagram shows the difference between what is observable to other people and what is out of sight to others:[16]

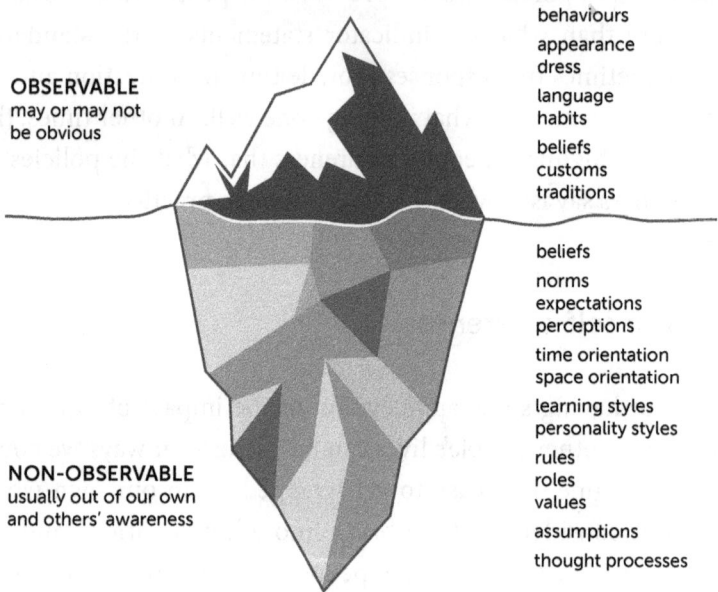

OBSERVABLE
may or may not
be obvious

behaviours
appearance
dress
language
habits
beliefs
customs
traditions

beliefs
norms
expectations
perceptions
time orientation
space orientation
learning styles
personality styles
rules
roles
values
assumptions
thought processes

NON-OBSERVABLE
usually out of our own
and others' awareness

Without self-awareness, auditors can easily impose their own beliefs and opinions on other people, who then go on to make significant changes in their own lives or workplaces.

I have come into contact with people anywhere up to five years after our first meeting in an audit and had them say to me, *'You know, Kathy, when you said xyz five years ago I was really thrown because I hadn't thought that any of those options could be possible. But I went away and did what you suggested and this is what changed as a result.'*

Sometimes I can't recall what I actually did say to the person when I first met them, especially when it was quite some time ago. When this sort of thing happens, I think about what my beliefs or opinions may have been at that time and sincerely trust that I have said and done the right thing for the person as well as for the organisation.

This approach reflects the principles identified in the widely known phrase 'first, do no harm' – or *'primum non nocere'*, the Latin translation from the original Greek – which means to not inflict harm intentionally. Aim to do good (beneficence) by providing benefits to persons and contributing to their welfare, and focusing on justice as well as respecting the person's autonomy. When difficult, real-time decisions must be made in an audit, it can be hard to apply the 'first, do no harm' approach because we really don't know what the actual risks and benefits may ultimately be, and our knowledge about what is in front of us at the time can be prone to error.

It is essential to remember that we can both overestimate what we think we know as well as underestimate our capacity to cause harm. It all comes back to our levels of awareness about how we operate, both as effective auditors and as human beings in general.

The role of feedback

Regularly seeking feedback from colleagues, team members and audited organisations can assist auditors to understand the impact of their words and actions on other people. Many auditors remain unaware of the effects of their approaches, perhaps because they have no real interest in knowing what these impacts may be on the organisation they are auditing or perhaps they don't want to change any aspect of their work practices.

Similarly, some people don't know what they don't know and are therefore unable to make changes to their work practices because they don't know to ask, or they don't hear or observe anything that conflicts with their opinions about themselves and what they do.

Feedback can assist us to be mindful of our ability to:

> operate with integrity and consideration
> be a good listener
> remain calm
> be in the moment with people
> be flexible in responding to situations and individuals
> keep things simple
> bring value to the situation and to the individuals involved
> continually challenge ourselves to improve our personal and professional approach
> not hold ourselves back
> not cover up bad news
> work through channels and pathways rather than go around them
> admit our mistakes.

So much to do, so little time!

Auditors perform many different roles in any audit situation, including:

> being able to rapidly assess a situation
> piecing together lots of information in a short time and seeing the opportunities as well as the weaknesses in the system
> engaging with many different people and rapidly building rapport
> looking for ways to solve problems with what they know or can find out
> being comfortable with using their intuition, dealing with ambiguity in different solutions
> adjusting rapidly to what is happening according to what is in front of them.

Effective auditors must bring a toolkit of different skills, knowledge and abilities to the audit, and not simply rely on a checklist to get them through.

In the final analysis, though, effective auditors practise their craft simultaneously and continuously. Auditors who meet that challenge often see their skills, abilities and knowledge strengthened and multiplied over time, and this is exactly what organisations and businesses require.

Reflections

Have you experienced a situation where people tell you what they have done as a result of something you said – perhaps years ago? What did you think when they told you? How did you feel?

....

....

....

....

In what ways do you examine your own beliefs and values?

....

....

....

....

Are you aware of how your own values and beliefs may influence the audit – and affect other people? What do you think could happen if you don't have this level of self-awareness?

....

....

....

....

Do you access formal feedback processes to build and refine your auditing practice? If not, why not?

....

....

....

....

Mentors often assist us to develop and refine our self-awareness and self-confidence. Do you have a mentor? If not, do you know someone who could be a good mentor for you?

....

....

....

....

....

....

....

....

....

....

7.

CEO EXPECTATIONS

Good leaders make sense of change in the world ... then imparts that insight to the team.
(DAN PENA)

As organisations progress further into a world where technology has an increased presence alongside greater client and community expectations, there is an escalating demand for auditors to focus on the forward-trending of risks and insights that lead to proactive quality assurance and regulatory compliance.

CEOs are frequently aware of the impact an audit or assessment can have on their organisation and its business. Some organisations relish the opportunity to demonstrate how they have made positive changes to address continual improvement within programs or across the business. In these instances, I often see audit outcomes openly shared with stakeholders and information provided to their clients. In most cases a productive audit can help the CEO, board members and staff experience insights that they may not have been able to see before – and, of course, learn more about the standards.

A lot depends on the organisation's baseline beliefs about what they are striving to achieve. For example, the focus of some organisations is clearly more on profit than on client outcomes, and some organisations may question the role of audits and why they are required. When the latter occurs, they may have been on the receiving end of questionable auditor practice in the past. These beliefs and experiences, whether stated or perhaps unconscious, may have become part of the organisation's culture or psyche, and can either make or break a positive auditing outcome.

What I have witnessed over the past decade is that most CEOs and organisations are well aware of the impact that different auditor types and styles can have on an audit outcome. CEOs have observed some auditors actively working on the compliance aspects of an audit as well as sharing information that could add value to the organisation over time.

Conversely, other auditors tend to work through the statements in the standards and get locked into details about a sub-section of an indicator, taking time away from reviewing and assessing progress made towards the overall standard or improvements the organisation had made since the previous audit process.

In some cases, the auditor may consciously or unconsciously use their position and authority to lord it over the CEO or staff and make their points more forcefully than is required. In this situation, staff as well as board members often go into damage control to work out ways to survive a process that is rarely constructive or helpful to the organisation as a whole. In these sorts of situations, CEOs state that only rarely are audits or assessments seen to be productive, insightful or helpful.

In my auditing and assessment work, I have worked with many people seeking a useful and impartial review of their organisation and its practices. However, there have been times when people have expressed extreme dissatisfaction or resentment about being expected to go through a process they view as demeaning, or where they don't agree with the purpose and intent of the standards in the first place. I have also worked in situations where the organisation goes through the process because it is something that they have to do in order to continue receiving much-needed funding – and so many opportunities can be lost when this approach isn't challenged in some way.

Frustrations

A lot of frustrations exist not only with the audit process itself, but also often with the reasons for being audited. Frustrations generally centre around:

> Cost
  - for the purchase of a quality management system relevant for the organisation or business
  - to pay for staff time to comprehend the standards
  - for staff to conduct internal audits
  - for consultants to assist in preparations or from whom systems can be purchased
  - to pay for the accreditation or certification audit.
> Time
  - to locate the correct system for the business or organisation
  - to develop and prepare the quality management system for audit
  - to locate the required evidence.

> The fallout from previous audits where poor experiences with auditors had occurred – and the fear of this happening again.

> Continued emphasis on 'ticking boxes' to address compliance, with the auditor not adding any other value to the business.

> Challenges in keeping up with legislative and regulatory changes as well as the continual review of standards from one year to the next.

> Existing government requirements to provide quarterly data, which is not seen to be enough to validate the organisation's commitment towards quality and client outcomes.

> Being expected to demonstrate continual improvement within business operations but without any real emphasis on potential opportunities for the business.

What frustration looks like

I have personally witnessed the impact of negative audit experiences on organisations and businesses. One situation involved a CEO's experiences with previous audits which had left him feeling demoralised and lacking in motivation for the current audit. When asked about this, he said his lack of enthusiasm was due to previous statements being made about his age and the length of time he had been working for the organisation. He said that comments had also been made about the currency of knowledge of some of his longstanding staff as well as about best practices in their sector and the capacity for both the staff and his organisation to demonstrate these practices for the audit. The

CEO described the previous audit experience as if it had only occurred the previous week when, in fact, it had been conducted almost 18 months earlier. The trauma described by this CEO sounded very real and was deeply concerning. He said he had worried about having the same auditor return.

CEOs have also explained situations where the previous auditor expressed a lot of personal opinions about the service and the state of the sector, without really listening to the experiences of the staff of the service that they were auditing at the time. These CEOs often say audits are known to be a fearful process for staff in their organisation and they dread the experience.

Imagine living with this and knowing all the while that the organisation is on a scheduled audit cycle, with dates for future audits known well in advance. Hearing these experiences makes me think of people living with the sword of Damocles over their head, living with the threat of danger each and every day they are at work. Imagine never being sure when the thread will be cut due to an accident or miscalculation because some form of evidence was not provided, or questions asked about the management of certain practices without any understanding of why the organisation has these approaches in place.

Personally, I don't believe anyone should be left so trauma-tised and damaged by an audit experience that they continue to carry this with them into the future of their organisation and its operations. This is not what an effective audit should provide. Yes, there is compliance involved – you can't get away from that – but there are also so many opportunities to acknowledge and draw out the positive effect the organisation or business is having on both its internal and external clients.

Examining frustration closely ...

What I have learned over the years is that frustration and anger can be indicators that something needs to be faced, whether within myself or within the organisation – or even both of us. After all, like everyone else, I have blind spots too! Over time, I have found it helpful to have another set of independent eyes look at what I am doing, both personally as well as in my businesses, and to identify not only where the gaps may be but also where things are on track. This approach has helped me to see where improvements need to be made so that I can do something about them.

Most people I meet during audits are seeking the best possible outcome for their organisation. However, the difference in results can come down to being prepared to ask for help, to courageously take the risk to hear what we may not want to hear, to trust in the process so that we can truly address things we don't understand – or where we don't know what we don't know.

In many ways, an external audit provides an ideal opportunity to reflect on and assess the past and then to use the acquired insights to inform the progression into the future. However, this is not a consistent experience for many organisations.

What I often witness is the impact on organisations when they lose staff because of their negative experiences with previous audit processes. This means that the organisation is continually dealing with internal change and disruption due to a lack of continuity amongst its key staff and hence a lack of consistency in how its internal systems are managed and maintained. Other staff can also become disengaged and disinterested when key staff leave. As a result, the impetus to continually review internal practices can be lost – and this is a far from ideal situation for any organisation to experience.

What the research says

Research conducted by KPMG states 68% of Australian CEOs believe their business is meeting and possibly exceeding client expectations.[17] Yet 60% of companies reported their auditor *did not* raise any issues or ideas that could be used in the business to enhance their processes or decisions.

In another study, where data was obtained over a 12-month period across a number of community organisations, questions arose about addressing the requirements of standards when the outcomes were not as strong as expected. For example, the data showed 51% of existing organisations had corrective actions to address, with 6% having notifiable issues, and in general 67% of the organisations with a major non-conformity *were not new* to the audit process.

The researchers explained that while organisations are striving to achieve certification, there are challenges in embedding quality systems and processes into their structures and operations. Incorporating the results from regular and rigorous review of the requirements of standards at both strategic and operational levels also appears to be a challenge.[18]

What I see in this research is that there is no mention about the role of education regarding what the standards and indicators mean, whether in local or online information sessions or during the actual audit process. I have often found the need to spend time educating people in amongst the audit process, particularly when it becomes apparent the interpretations made by the organisation or business are not current with what the standards require – or where the sector has made best practice improvements and the organisation has not addressed these within its practices.

I also found that when people express anger about improvement actions I identified for their audit, there was often a mismatch between their interpretation of the standards and what was actually required. I understand their disappointment, particularly when a lot of effort had gone into developing and maintaining the quality system throughout the year.

What organisations can ask for

There are so many opportunities for CEOs and organisations to consider not only what they need to achieve from the audit process, but also to actively consider the type of auditor they will require for the audit.

While it is common practice for organisations to seriously consider the reputation and scope of the certification body for their audits, with checklists being in place solely for this purpose, it is often unclear what other thought may have gone into the preparations for the audit. For example:

> Apart from carefully considering the certification body requirements and the 'fit' with their organisation, have key staff thought about what auditor attributes and knowledge might be useful to their organisation?

> Do organisations look at the credentials of the auditor beyond a general overview? For example, do they ask for a CV to look at other experiences that the auditor might bring to the audit?

> Do organisations use internet searches to see what information there is about the auditor on the internet or social media?

> ➤ Have key staff sought references from other organisations
> about who they had for their audit? Was their audit a
> useful, 'ho-hum' or detrimental experience?

When audits are conducted by government regulators, organisations and businesses do not have a choice about who the auditor will be. However, for other types of audits, organisations and businesses may seek to engage auditors of their choice. These auditors may have conducted audits for the organisation in the past or they may have specific skill sets required by the organisation for their audit. In some cases, self-aware and effective Expert Auditors or Ambassador Auditors will be sought because of their ability to provide valuable insights into the organisation's business operations.

However, at all times, organisations should feel confident about the auditor's experience, credentials, reputation and approach. Research[19] tells us that other professions and international agencies are seeking auditors who operate beyond a mainstream compliance framework or a tick-box mindset. I believe the human services sector should be no different, and CEOs searching for an exemplary audit experience should be mindful of the level of auditor engaged.

Not everything that counts can be counted, and not everything that can be counted counts.
(WILLIAM BRUCE CAMERON)

Reflections

What do you think are the greatest challenges facing CEOs and organisations today?

....

....

....

....

....

....

....

How do you think CEOs and organisations respond when an auditor does not raise any issues or provide them with useful ideas from their audit?

....

....

....

....

....

....

....

In what ways can an auditor address the frustrations expressed or exhibited by a CEO or organisation about an audit?

....

....

....

....

....

....

....

Does your online presence match what you stand for and represent? Is your CV worth sharing?

....

....

....

....

....

....

....

....

8.

A WORLD WITHOUT AUDITING?

Is it possible to have a world without auditing?

While I know that people often feel like audits and certification or accreditation assessments are a significant imposition in their work life, the reality is that audits and assessments have been a part of our world since ancient times in civilizations such as those in China, Egypt and Greece.

The word 'audit' was originally derived from the Latin term '*audire*' which means 'to hear'. Researchers have learned that auditors in these ancient times were required to orally report to officials and business owners or people in higher positions of authority about the status of progress or about the tallies of products. With the introduction of written language, the auditor's role subsequently evolved to include the verification of written records and, in some cases, to be the ears in the community.

Gaining traction in the 1930s, an increased interest in quality was supported by a steady evolution in thought leadership as well as the integration of ideas and subsequent spread of knowledge across countries and sectors.[20] This required the development of systems thinking and the involvement of auditors in reviewing, auditing and assessing management systems that involved entire organisations, from governance, finances and HR through to addressing clients' needs.

As strategies to refine quality became known, many opportunities to share ideas and practices, not only within industries, but also across sectors became possible. While auditing has been primarily associated with the financial world, the service industry sector and the not-for-profit world have also become familiar with the role and impact of standards in their organisational practices. The approach taken by service industries encompasses both predictable work practices and, more importantly, an emphasis on satisfying the individual client at the point of service transaction.

During the latter decades of 20th century, the Australian Government developed its own expectations about input and outputs, seeking details about funded organisations' financial conditions and uniformity of practices. Audits are now a statutory requirement for most human services organisations operating throughout Australia.

Since the early 2000s, the Australian Government as well as state governments have mostly collaborated with the non-government sector to address the standards expected of services and organisations providing supports to vulnerable people – as well as to develop assessment processes that review performance against a relevant set of standards.

For virtually all standards applying to the human services sector, there is an expectation that people in receipt of those services have the right to participate in the identification and implementation of continual service improvements and to expect the organisation to be meeting, and possibly exceeding, nominated standards.

Could a world without audits be possible?

But what would happen if we didn't have any audits or assessment processes at all? What would that look like? I suspect we would operate in an environment with no checks or balances on what we do, no accountability measures in place to monitor the impacts of actions, deeds or words on both our internal as well as external clients. We might see a world where anarchy prevailed: anarchy as a utopian society where individuals enjoy complete freedom without government – or, more likely, anarchy as a state of disorder due to the absence or non-recognition of authority or any other controlling system. In this sort of world, societies might remain intact and even thrive under alternatives to traditional hierarchies – but the question is, for how long?

What is interesting is that some research suggests that businesses and organisations would be better off without the burden of compliance and that a 'risk-adjusted approach that removes the compliance burden for trusted organisations with a strong record' would go a long way in enabling innovation and responsiveness to changing needs.[21] While this sounds like an admirable goal, what this would look like in practice is not clear. For example, subsequent audit outcomes for long-standing and perceived strong organisations or businesses may be accompanied by a number of improvement actions, perhaps because of a change of senior staff, change of business direction or a loss of vision about what the organisation or business should be doing.

Auditing as the 'dark side'

Welcome to the dark side —
where all the fun stuff happens!
(@ REBEL CIRCUS)

I often hear colleagues working for community-based organisations say they would be a lot better off without audits. They frequently express concern about what is happening across different sectors as well as about some of the challenges organisations experience when addressing change. Yet, amongst these challenging times, there are opportunities to be had, new things to try, better ways to make progress, ways to buck the usual trends.

And then they make the comment: '*Oh Kathy, what on earth are you doing? We are doing all we can to make a difference, while you have well and truly gone to the dark side!*'

While I know full well that none of these people understand why I believe my auditing work to be so important, I also know that they see very little point to their organisation being audited, apart from the tangible links with ongoing funding. They often talk about their view of auditing: the burden of it all, having to do things that don't make any real sense, the imposition on the organisation or business, the diversion of staff from performing their considerably more important duties to doing something related to 'quality' (whatever that is!), the financial costs and time needed to prepare for the audit as well as being expected to spend time and effort to address things that are not right or as strong as they need to be to meet particular standards after the audit has been completed.

Where did the idea of the 'dark side' come from?

The origin of the 'dark side' comment is based on the evil and malevolent aspect of both human personality and society as a whole. In religious imagery, for example, the 'light' side is often representative of God, heaven and the angels, whereas the 'dark' side is often referred to as evil, sin and the Devil respectively.

However, when my colleagues make this sort of statement, I know it is being made in a light-hearted and somewhat comical context. While they humorously tell me that I have 'gone over to the dark side', I know I am quite at ease with the fact that I have opted – and actually prefer – something that is out of fashion or not a social group's accepted preference.

I think the 'dark side' is spot-on for me as an auditor. I am a *Star Wars* fan from way back, and what my friends don't see is that truly value-added and insightful audits and assessments provide so many opportunities for organisations to see not only the strengths of what they do but also areas which may present unnecessary weaknesses to them.

When you look at the dark side, careful you must be.
For the dark side looks back.
(YODA)

Thinking about the Death Star that was built in the 1983 movie *Return of the Jedi* and, in particular, what happened when the one key weakness for that huge satellite was found, there are many parallels to be had between this situation and the ones we see in an audit.

For example, we can truly believe that what we are doing is amazing, indestructible and invincible (the Empire's view of themselves as well as of the huge size and might of the Death Star), but it may take only one seemingly innocuous, small thing (the structural weakness identified in the thermal exhaust port) to eventually blow us out of the water (Luke Skywalker's precise hit into the small exhaust shaft that triggered a chain reaction for the detonation to occur and the complete destruction of the Death Star).

Parallels between the destruction of the Death Star and audits in today's world

Parallels to the destruction of the Death Star can readily be seen in many organisations and businesses in areas such as:

> discrepancies between what the governing body think the organisation is about and what the organisation actually does
> the organisation seeking feedback from its clients and then not listening to them or ignoring what they are saying because 'we know best'
> ego-driven attitudes and approaches implemented by people managing the business
> not keeping abreast of legislative, regulatory and mandated requirements
> cutting corners with service delivery practices
> ignoring the human rights of staff as well as clients
> stating the organisation provides a reputable and safe accommodation setting for vulnerable people when

their staff do not report situations where abuse is happening.

This list could go on and on.

Where were the Death Star auditors?

Reflecting on the demise of the Death Star, one would have to wonder why *they* (being the builders, commanders, etc.) weren't aware of such a fundamental flaw. Surely *someone* (perhaps an auditor or two!) would have pointed out the flaw was there? But as we see from the Death Star's eventual destruction, apparently *nobody* did anything about the flaw and the result was the significant loss of life (whether they were on the 'right' or the 'wrong' side!), a massive waste of money to build something that could be so easily destroyed and, of course, a reprieve for the story's heroes.

Unfortunately, flaws in well-intended practices do occur and they present challenges, not only for the organisation or business involved, but also for the government and funding body and their expectations about the outcomes of service delivery for vulnerable people. The reality is that governments also review how organisations and businesses comply with standards.

What's intriguing about the role of audits is that these are often conducted by external specialists who can identify potential flaws. In many situations where flaws or improvement actions are identified, there have been no other ways for the organisation to listen to a different type of 'truth'. The fresh set of eyes was needed. Usually, organisations greatly appreciate being made aware of the potential for unforeseen destruction and the fallout costs that can then be prevented.

I believe the work that goes into developing and implementing an organisation that can be and should be sustainable over time is something well worth investing in. Knowing where potential pitfalls or flaws are so that something can be done to rectify or mitigate them just makes sense.

The evolving audit arena (or future-proofing the Death Star)

Focusing on compliance is one thing, but it shouldn't be the only task that is addressed in an audit. Adding value and working side by side with people to see potential opportunities and identify potential gaps in achieving the long-term strategic aims of an organisation or business should be more strongly defined in auditing practices.

Audits or assessments quite rightly continue to challenge the robustness of the internal controls and processes an organisation has in place, giving an external perspective and the provision of valuable feedback. We are also seeing audits and assessments taking a stronger role in 'future-proofing' organisations and supporting strategies that provide assurances of trust, integrity and transparency of business practices to clients.

The world of businesses and organisations is changing and evolving – but is the auditing arena evolving at the same pace? From my experience as an auditor and assessor listening to people's frustrations about audits, I believe there is scope for the auditing industry to learn from organisations and businesses that are actively preparing for technological advances, such as the more common uses of apps and tools, changes to the way people will work in future as well as the ways our Gen Ys and

Gen Zs will look at today's organisations and businesses in five to ten years' time. Will their requirements and worldview be the same as ours?

We can also learn from the way society expects organisations and their staff to have a defined and visible social purpose, as well as organisations being far more accountable and transparent to their stakeholders and clients. Similarly, we auditors need to be looking at the impact of ongoing compliance on different sectors. We need to be listening to organisations and businesses that want other ways to demonstrate how they are seeking to be innovative and responsive as well as successful and sustainable over time.

What we auditors can do

As an auditor, I think there are several things that we can do:

1. Don't make assumptions – about anything.
2. Be a role model that talks the talk and walks the walk – all the time, not just when you are visible or in front of other people.
3. Set the standard – and be seen to consistently operate at that level.
4. Look for ways to get buy-in from all levels across the organisation.
5. Look for solutions to the issues you see – and ask other people to do the same.
6. Perform regular check-ups and do some spot checks – including of your own work practices.
7. Praise performance and acknowledge a job well done.

Perhaps the questions we should be asking now could focus on why audits and assessments continue to be seen in a mostly negative light. Perhaps it is time to debate and challenge perspectives such as people not believing they and/or their organisation should be reviewed at all. Perhaps alternatives are waiting in the wings to be discovered and acted upon to take our world forward into the 2020s and beyond.

Regardless, the world without any form of auditing or assessing doesn't appear to be likely any time soon. Going forward, auditors may increasingly be required to step up and refine their approach, going beyond the compliance-focused mindset. In some cases, this will be an exciting challenge for both the auditor and the organisation, whereas for other people this will require intense personal courage.

However, when auditors are confronted by situations where organisations and their staff actively collude in human rights breaches, cover up inappropriate practice or do not take a stand about the rights of internal or external clients, it is not always easy for an auditor to step up and act on what the evidence presents. This is where the auditor must exhibit courage and uphold the accountabilities located not only in the documented standards, but also within ethical practice standards. The auditor must demonstrate diligent duty of care responsibilities and have the courage and fortitude to hold tough conversations with the CEO, board members or external authorities. Regardless of the potential or actual threats made about what you are exposing, turning a blind eye just doesn't cut it!

From what I have seen, courageous auditors actively explore and expose not only the dark side of organisations and the impact of their practices, but also praise the professional practices and innovations that enhance client experiences and expectations.

Courageous auditors have so many opportunities to acknowledge best practice and to applaud actions taken by organisations and businesses to meet the requirements of professional business and service delivery practice standards. Our reports provide those opportunities, as do discussions and regular feedback during the audit process about practices that encourage best practice as well as opportunities to learn from what other similar entities have done well.

Reflections

Have you thought about a world without any auditing? What would that look like for you?

....

....

....

....

In what ways do you add value and work alongside the organisation and its people during an audit?

....

....

....

....

How can you assist CEOs and organisations to view audits in a positive and useful way?

....

....

....

....

Are you a courageous auditor?

....

....

....

....

In what ways do you respond when confronted by the dark side
of an organisation or business practice?

....

....

....

....

Conversely, in what ways do you highlight and promulgate better
practices?

....

....

....

....

9

THE FUTURE OF AUDITING

*Fear of the unknown will always be overpowered
by human desire toward exploration. Curiosity
is the risk whose gift often pays off.*

(MLADEN ĐORĐEVIĆ)

Over the past six years I have seen Australian organisations providing disability services grapple with the changes required to move from a welfare-oriented framework to a market-driven service economy as the impact of the National Disability Insurance Scheme (NDIS) becomes more apparent to their strategic and operational structures. The loss of block funding, where the service could allocate funds where it saw the most need to an environment where the person with disability has control of their own funds and the ability to purchase services and supports as they choose has created fear and tension in some services. Conversely, in other services the NDIS has gifted the opportunity to work in a very different way with people with disabilities.

The various Australian state governments alerted the community service sector of the changes ahead of time and provided support to manage the transition. Some services relished the opportunity to make the required changes and implement new strategies that would enhance their operations and reputations.

The CEO of one service I audited during this period said that once she had realised the potential of the NDIS and the move to a market-driven service model, she actively encouraged staff as well as clients to see the positive benefits associated with the change. The management committee welcomed the opportunity to direct the change at the strategic governance level.

During interviews over this period, I would be asked at each audit how their service was going in comparison to other services in their sector: services they now saw as their competitors. While I could not provide that level of insight, regardless of their efforts to elicit these details from me, the interviews over this period highlighted the personal actions taken by individual management committee members to progress the changes at the highest level of the service – and this was also apparent at senior management and operational staff levels as well.

Gone were the days where the client was not informed about their funding situation. Between one audit and the next, services and their staff frequently demonstrated how they now worked closely with the people with disabilities to educate and support them to understand the funding and staff management practices.

Interviews with people with disabilities throughout this period also showed their growing awareness of how the service itself operated, and the many benefits they enjoyed as a result of being viewed as a person in control of their own life. Many people with disabilities said they were no longer dictated to by a service that did not understand what they required to live a good life.

During that same period, I audited other services that really struggled with the changes. Concerns were mostly related to the financial uncertainty in delivering services to vulnerable people while, at the same time, continuing with the same structures they had enjoyed before the changes commenced. Some people could not comprehend the new processes where the person with disability has control of their funds and is able to direct the services they receive from the organisation's workers. Board members sometimes found it challenging to progress from a charity mindset to one where the organisation needed to operate more like a commercial business.

Audits with one service during this period highlighted these challenges, with some people resisting the audit process as well. Interviews with management committee members and staff highlighted the efforts people were making to work out how the service could continue to operate as it had with block funding and with existing structures. Change was not envisaged; instead, the focus was 'service delivery as usual'.

Interviews with people with disabilities often told a different story, however. During each subsequent audit of this organisation during this same period, people with disabilities occasionally expressed dissatisfaction with their existing service and I was told that as soon as they had their own personal NDIS plan, they would be looking around for alternative service providers and then leaving. Even though these people were telling the service of their frustrations, this did not mean the service would take this feedback seriously. For example, at subsequent audits, I often found long-term clients had indeed left and the impact on the service was quite marked.

Throughout this period of transition, I was continually mindful of my role as an auditor, not only in terms of addressing the stated compliance requirements, but also in keeping abreast of the changes and impacts of the NDIS on services and individuals as well as the impact of continually evolving business practices. I have found that 'walking with' people during these audits frequently involves having an extensive set of knowledge and tools to draw upon, not just those related to the audit procedures and methods. Examples of knowledge that I drew upon include:

> the wide range and impact of changes in organisational behaviour
> business management as well as business process improvement strategies
> risk management strategies, including risk identification and assessment processes
> relevant legal, legislative, regulatory and contractual practices
> the range of organisational contexts and tools used for strategic planning
> conflict resolution practices and skills
> quality management principles, tools and improvement techniques
> operations and service management practices
> the types of technology used by organisations
> leadership practices
> the role of ethical integrity and professionalism
> the difference between a mainstream audit and compliance-focus mentality and the role of assessing and future-proofing organisational effectiveness.

Organisations want more from the audit process

As the 2020s continue to unfold, we can see that organisations are evolving at an increasingly rapid rate and 'business as usual' appears to be losing its effectiveness in a time of marked technological change. In contrast to only a decade ago, and like the evolution into the NDIS environment, people are working differently, are motivated differently and have different expectations today than those they held not so long ago.

Building, implementing and maintaining organisations and workforces that can manage the need for agility, responsiveness and continued attention to addressing client requirements demands something more of businesses and their leaders – it demands courage to bring people along on the journey; courage to build something better for the business; courage to meet the different needs of the workforce and clients; courage to invest in technology and strategies that have not been attempted before; courage to leave a legacy. At times, it can feel like navigating new territory without a map!

To help provide the roadmap, the role of auditors and assessors is being called upon to evolve and change as well. Research conducted by Forbes Insights and KPMG states businesses want auditors to 'operate more like a partner' and provide insights that the business may not be aware of so to enable the organisation to manage the business more effectively – and, in some cases, more competitively.[22] This research also indicates that businesses, including providers of human services, are looking for auditors to provide specific observations and recommendations that can add value – not just a 'laundry list of ideas' and to 'take things to the next level' through actionable information for the organisation.

Auditor continuity between one audit and the next is also viewed positively, particularly when the auditor develops a deep understanding of the business and its essential as well as less important operations and is aware of the business's competitors and the role of other organisations in their industry.

Over the past decade, I have heard CEOs increasingly demand this level of attention within an audit, as well as an amplified focus on the forward-trending of risks and insights that lead to both proactive quality assurance as well as regulatory compliance. These changes suggest auditors are required to have more business and governance skills and abilities than they may have required in previous years, and this is confirmed in research where 93% of respondents believed 'the audit profession needs to evolve'.[23]

Audit implications for an organisation or business

Regardless of whether it is an internal or external process, audits are costly in terms of time and disruption to workflow, particularly with lost productivity and time away from usual tasks for staff to organise the requirements for the process.

Many organisations have their own internal audit sections or quality management staff to review the standards and address what these mean in relation to their business operations throughout the year. People managing internal audits generally report directly to the board and senior management and provide regular reviews of internal functions and practices across the organisation. Internal audits also provide assurances that the business's governance, risk management and operational practices are functioning as they should.

Where there are identified issues or non-compliances with these processes, recommendations are made to resolve these within designated timeframes and to make ongoing improvements designed to enhance the business's operations. In addition, organisations frequently have the capacity to evaluate the effectiveness of their audit system and methodology to ensure their planning, reporting, recording, analysing, implementing and monitoring practices lead to improved results.[24]

While there are clear benefits, undertaking any form of audit or assessment has a financial cost to an organisation, either in terms of staff time to prepare and undertake the audit or in the cost of meeting with external assessors and preparing for certification processes for the organisation to comply with a range of standards applicable to their industry.

Audit quality

In my role as an auditor and assessor, I continue to be confronted by a range of perceptions about the quality and impact of audits on organisations and businesses. For example, audits are often viewed positively as:

1. an appreciated and welcome review of their practices and systems
2. helpful and providing practical insights into strengthening business operations and service delivery practices
3. a valued process that enhances internal practices
4. a process that can be validated by external best practices
5. an opportunity to reflect on what is done well – and to

search for ways to continually improve what is being done now

6. not just about compliance but about the organisation's long-term journey.

Or alternatively, audits are viewed negatively as:

1. an imposed function (a 'necessary evil') to obtain and/or retain funding
2. only about risk and compliance, not opportunities for improvement
3. an expensive function that does not add any value to the organisation or its operations
4. a waste of time and resources, particularly when the auditors do not make any observations to guide future decision-making that the organisation needs to remain current and viable within a continually changing environment
5. an out-of-date function that contributes the business lagging behind the dizzying pace of business and regulatory changes
6. increasingly irrelevant in the drive for compliance, particularly when actual quality and how this can be demonstrated within outcomes does not appear to be seen valued or appreciated
7. problematic due to previous experiences associated with ego or personality clashes with the auditor.

From what I can see, audits should ideally be:

> conducted by auditors with a deep appreciation of the organisation and its operations
> relevant and meaningful
> insightful
> a comprehensive value-added experience
> a confirmation that the organisation is attempting to comply with the relevant standards applicable to their operations – even when there are improvements that the organisation may need to make
> conducted in such a way that effective partnerships and strong levels of trust can develop.

However, the reality for organisations is that they may not experience these quality outcomes. When external auditors only use a tick-box approach, an organisation may be left in a position where they are no better informed than when the audit began. Instead they will have spent a lot of time and money on something they could already access themselves through their internal audit processes. Similarly, when organisations are confronted with auditors who lack experience in the organisation's industry, poor and potentially expensive outcomes may be apparent.

It is true that there are no universally agreed upon definitions of high- or low-quality audits, meaning it can be challenging for organisations and businesses to accurately judge audit quality. The elements for conducting audits are quite complex and difficult to measure, particularly when people are not aware of the various rules governing the process. In fact, a considerable amount of the audit practice is virtually invisible and mostly unknown to organisations being audited. Moreover, organisations may not be aware that auditors are expected to maintain currency with their practice and to address various quality and peer review processes.

From what I have seen, organisations frequently assess the audit based on the auditor who is conducting the audit, and will determine that the audit quality has been poor because of factors related to the auditor's performance, issues with the auditor's knowledge and approach, as well as issues after the audit has finished, such as the timely receipt and clarity of reports, and the provision of appropriate information to guide the way forward.

Conversely, a high-quality audit provides not only a systematic and objective assessment of an organisation's strategic and operational practices, but frequently also gives a true and fair snapshot view of the way the organisation is currently functioning. Risks may be discussed, with recommendations to resolve potential as well as current issues, and opportunities may also be raised. Similarly, audit reports following a high-quality audit provide logical, deep and clear insights into where and organisation or business is strong and where further opportunities abound.

As a general principle, organisations need to be assured that their auditor has delivered an appropriate professional opinion supported by sufficient evidence and objective judgements obtained throughout the audit, to address not only the compliance requirements of the standards, but to add value to the organisation as well.

What this means for auditors

But what does it take to progress from a being a tick-box auditor to an auditor who is skilled and well-known for their professional auditing and assessing practice? How can auditors focus more on a high-quality audit outcome as their standard practice? What does it take to make this progression? And is it really important that auditors provide far more than a focus on compliance in an audit?

From what I have seen over the past decade, it is not until the auditor themselves realises that something about their practice needs to change that progress is achieved. To benefit from this sort of realisation, the auditor has to identify and 'own' what needs to be acted upon for improvement. I think it often takes significant personal courage to acknowledge that our approach may need to adapt and improve, not only on terms of the audit tasks, but also our ability to successfully communicate with CEOs, board members and other stakeholders during both straightforward and challenging audits.

From what I have seen of auditors who excel at their role, the ability to seek feedback from their peers and be open to continually learn appear to be critical components towards improved practice. The acknowledgement that they don't – and can't – know everything also appears to be important! Similarly, seeking mentors who work with and provide significant insights that are heard and acted upon are often utilised by auditors who excel at their practice.

The reality is that today's auditors are increasingly expected to keep pace with the changes occurring in the business world – or risk stagnation. This means not only keeping abreast of these changes, but also actively seeing where businesses and organisations may be impacted upon by these events. Sharing information and website links about different practices, including those in other sectors dissimilar to the organisation being audited, can help people to challenge their own thinking and perceptions about what is possible. Similarly, sharing information about relevant research and networks is often gratefully accepted by key staff, who may not have the time to look for other types of information.

In this way, auditors take on a distinctive role within the audit process, progressing beyond a 'maintainer-controller'[25] mindset that CEOs and organisations so often see within an auditing process. Many board members and CEOs seek an audit approach where they learn more, not only about the standards, but also about practices that could assist their organisation in its quest towards best practice. And this is where an auditor can truly excel and contribute towards organisational improvements over time.

Reflections

Do you think your audit organisations regard you as having good knowledge and experience in the industry? Is there more you can do?

....

....

....

....

....

....

How do you think you can keep abreast of technological change and retain currency in an ever-changing world? What do you do now? Could you do more?

....

....

....

....

....

....

....

In what ways do you try to perform like a partner in an audit process? Does this approach work?

....

....

....

....

....

....

....

In what ways do you challenge your own thinking? Is this different to how you challenge other people's thinking?

....

....

....

....

....

....

....

....

10.

THE ROLE OF THE EXPERT AUDITOR

The expert in anything was once a beginner.
(RUTHERFORD B HAYES)

LEVELS	TYPE	FOCUS	POSITION	RESULT	VALUE
LEVEL 5	AMBASSADOR	LEVERAGE	INFLUENCER	STRENGTH	+90%+
LEVEL 4	EXPERT	INSIGHT	PRODUCER	VALUE	+70%
LEVEL 3	LEAD	COMPLIANCE	GUIDE	ASSURANCE	+40%
LEVEL 2	SUPPORT	COMPETENCE	CONTRIBUTOR	ASSISTANCE	-10%
LEVEL 1	NOVICE	SYSTEM	FOLLOWER	INVISIBLE	-20%

Lead Auditors with extensive industry experience are often known as Expert Auditors, particularly when they have worked in the same industry as the standards they are assessing and have developed a range of insights into the ways organisations operate. Expert Auditors bring detailed technical knowledge of organisational management issues from their own experience working at senior levels within government or in the business or community services sector. With this type of knowledge, they can delve into the strategic and operational systems for organisations and 'talk the talk'. They are able to provide insight into what the standards mean in a practical way and explain what is required in a relevant organisational context.

Based on their longstanding professional experience, Expert Auditors frequently operate in a strongly ethical and decisive manner, using a range of open-minded, observant, perceptive, versatile, culturally sensitive and collaborative skills within an audit process. Expert Auditors who have strong 'people skills' will want to get along well with people, while at the same time be able to take a 'hard stand' because of their integrity and knowledge about how the sector works. They are capable of handling negative feedback without taking it personally, mostly because they have personal value systems in place.

While they continue to focus on strategies that fulfil their auditing duty, Expert Auditors will not shy away from making meaningful observations or having difficult conversations. They routinely use tactful and diplomatic measures to mount a compelling case for their points.

While the relationship between the Expert Auditor and the organisation may be challenging to manage, ultimately organisations benefit from the insights they provide, particularly when the Expert Auditor has considerable knowledge and depth of understanding about the organisation and the sector in which it operates. For example, Expert Auditors often provide independent yet detailed opinion on the organisation's business operations as well as what needs to be done to rectify or strengthen its practices, whether through improvement actions, observations or discussion. The challenge for the Expert Auditor may well be in how to create a partnership with the organisation during the audit and, at the same time, remain independent.

The traits espoused by professional Expert Auditors are essential to the integrity of the audit process. In addressing key issues within the audit process, Expert Auditors are known to be articulate with many different stakeholders and have the skills to encourage people to take positive action as a result of the audit. These people are attentive to detail, meticulous when reviewing evidence against particular indicators and, as a result, often do not settle for the easy answer.

Consistent adherence to these traits ensures that the audit results will be reliable, robust and a benefit to the organisation. It also ensures the perpetuation of the audit process as a positive experience for all concerned. Expert Auditors also aim to provide insightful discussion within the audit process and provide clarity about beneficial outcomes for the organisation.

The really expert riders of horses let the horse know immediately who is in control, but then guide the horse with loose reins and seldom use the spurs.

(SANDRA DAY O'CONNOR)

Reflections

Do you think that people can learn to be an Expert Auditor or is this a level that can only be attained by people who have existing expertise?

....

....

....

....

....

....

Are there are other challenges for an Expert Auditor apart from remaining independent in an audit process? If so, how do you think these challenges can be managed?

....

....

....

....

....

....

....

What other benefits do you consider an Expert Auditor could bring to an audit?

....

....

....

....

....

....

....

Do you believe that you could be an Expert Auditor? What would you do to evidence this capability?

....

....

....

....

....

....

....

....

11.

AUDITING IN 2025 & BEYOND ...

Be fearless. Have the courage to take risks. Go where there are no guarantees. Get out of your comfort zone even if it means being uncomfortable. The road less traveled is sometimes fraught with barricades, bumps and uncharted terrain. But it is on that road where your character is truly tested. Have the courage to accept that you're not perfect. Nothing is and no one is — and that's OK.

(KATIE COURIC)

As we face the impact of technological changes to the way auditing generally operates, the increased use of artificial intelligence and alternative forms of communicating are becoming more apparent for the business operations of small, medium and large organisations. Research states that artificial intelligence is guiding decisions on anything from crop dusting to bank loans, and predictions are firmly in place for totally automated client services across a range of sectors in the not-too-distant future.[26] However, technology is not the biggest challenge for organisations and businesses – culture is.

The role of artificial intelligence

Artificial intelligence is already operating in our lives today. We have ready access to mobile phones and we can share documents virtually and instantly from wherever we are located to other places in the world. Similarly, we can download information at the touch of a button. This technology has seen us make great strides forward in the ways we do our work.

Surveys have been conducted across the world to look at the impact of technology on workplace stress and, unsurprisingly, 70% of workers in one survey stated they want more technology, not less – particularly in areas that replace manual and laborious tasks.[27] Some 55% of workers wanted their employers to use more automation technology such as artificial intelligence. Many workers have asked for better technology to help them to work more effectively – and this is no different for auditors and assessors, as well as the organisations being audited and assessed.

When artificial intelligence is broadly integrated into daily work operations, employees are often able to use the algorithms' recommendations to supplement their own decisions. And, of course, we are seeing the impact of artificial intelligence in communications we receive from online interactions.

For example, I regularly purchase e-books from one supplier and I have been watching with a good deal of interest how the site is progressively working out which books would be a good match for me. I am informed that the matching efforts can be up to 95% accurate – interesting! – until I decide to randomly buy a completely different type of book just to see what the algorithm makes of that!

You just have to consider how quickly a search on your mobile phone – or even a photo you have taken – results in social media feeds. This is what is happening now, even when it is not explicit in our organisational or business culture or within our conscious awareness.

Connections between artificial intelligence and auditing

Research conducted by the World Economic Forum indicates that by 2025, 30% of corporate audits will be conducted by AI (artificial intelligence).[28] Considering the future for auditing, Forbes research indicates auditors will need to become savvier with the role and use of technology as we progress further into the 2020s and beyond.[29]

While audits generally involve the review of documentation and interviews with a wide range of people, we are rapidly reaching the point at which AI is taking over the general review of policies and procedures using hundreds of thousands, if not millions, of data points to obtain a clear insight into what these documents should have in place. With this type of automated technology, auditors will be able to identify and review a client's processes and, through the use of process mining, explore them in depth.[30]

On the other hand, as organisations and businesses become more adept at using AI, they will be able to work around and potentially manipulate information so that the documentation provided in an audit appears to be correct. We see this approach being used with search engine optimisation (SEO), which involves the increased visibility of information or words to search engine users. While SEO is interested in increasing the numbers of 'right' words so that search result ranking is improved, it doesn't matter whether the words are 'right' in practice or not. Auditors will need to be able to see through this 'optimisation' during document reviews and focus on what really matters in relation to an organisation's business. This is particularly important in audits where the organisation has purchased an 'off-the-shelf' policy and procedure manual: the words may be right but the substance in the ways the organisation interprets and implements these practices may be missing.

While the fundamental processes contained within any audit or assessment are not expected to change, the use of new technologies and automation has the capacity to free up auditors' time and provide the opportunity for human judgement, continued professional scepticism as well as the use of soft skills and improved communication techniques – something that only a human being can do (at this time!).

As the studies by Forbes note, CEOs are actively seeking more insights into strengthening their operations and want more visible added value from an audit – which can be obtained from auditors who bring specific knowledge and tools to address governance and business management practices.

Auditor proficiency, not only with data analysis, but more specifically in the use of critical thinking and judgement will become increasingly more important for forthcoming audits. This will need to be accompanied by the ability to constructively challenge management practices and work across various domains. It is certainly possible that these practices could be effectively supplemented by artificial intelligence and would ideally provide client organisations with a strong and productive outcome. But only time will tell!

What the futurists have to say

In recent years, futurists have been vocal about the diverse ways organisations are preparing for the future and the role human knowledge is having in driving these changes forward. According to one futurist, research around this topic suggests that while it took a century in the past for human knowledge to double, human knowledge has doubled within one year.[31] This was achieved in 2020, and predictions of knowledge doubling within 12 hours have been forecast for the year 2030.

This has left me wondering how people will be able to assimilate so much knowledge in a rapidly evolving world of technology and changes with the way we work. Running in parallel with adapting to this level of knowledge acquisition and technological evolution (such as artificial intelligence, instant access to apps for many different uses, augmented reality, neuro-technology and the impact of 'big data') we might see the need for an update to human values and capacity. Humanity may need assistance to cope with, and address, such far-reaching changes and maintain a sense of human wellbeing amid so much of what could be – or is – ahead of us.

Futurists aim to build effective strategies from a range of different perspectives. These include a number of responses to the key issues confronting an organisation or business, and then look at not only what needs to be *done* from now on, but also what must *stop*.

From an auditor's perspective, most strategic plans I see in an audit hardly ever focus beyond what needs to be actioned in the next year or two (I rarely see plans for five years or longer) to take into account the attitudes and functions that need to cease *now* to make those longer term opportunities workable. Most often, the required actions are considered in conjunction with what is currently happening, while defined changes in the crucial but less tangible factors like attitude or culture are rarely expected. Similarly, actions that must be stopped and replaced do not often appear in these strategic plans.

Strategy building

From what I can see, effective strategy building definitely involves courage: courage to look at and address potential scenarios that we may not want to face or situations that we can't even imagine could be possible in some cases. For example, research I conducted in 2013 found that there were very few human services strategic plans and responses that planned for people to control and manage their own funding or to engage their own disability support workers.[32] The few services that had embraced the right of people to take control of their own lives were regarded by mainstream organisations as 'mavericks' and 'trouble-makers'. Yet by 2020 this approach has become common throughout Australia, with many existing and new service providers absorbing this model into their service delivery practices.

Effective strategy building gives us permission to think the unthinkable, to envisage quite different possibilities and to open up different ways of doing things. For example, the way we view food is continually changing and there are ways people can see, with the use of a low-cost device, the origin and age of food. In other situations, technology is being used on plants to internally activate its own resistance to pests and disease instead of using chemicals. These actions and initiatives have been made because traditional points of view about progressing forward were suspended and alternative options encouraged and trialled.

Impact of technological change on audits

Hearing and seeing the extent of technological changes that are already happening across organisations and businesses – plus what is being projected for the next decade – is both sobering and exciting at the same time. It is sobering when I think about the challenges organisations and businesses experience in developing relevant plans to address the future but then find their plans may simply be a continuation of past achievements or a derivative of what the organisation believes the funding body expects. Sometimes strategic plans reflect an organisation's stubborn commitment towards maintaining traditions and rituals at all costs.

Continuing these practices in the face of the impact of technology and other changes can result in an organisation's gradual demise. Granted, these traditions provide people with a sense of belonging and a connection with the organisation's history. However, if this is all they do, the opportunities to use these traditions and rituals to continually build and refine the organisation's agility and relevance may mean opportunities and relevant future planning activities can be lost.[33]

Thinking about the number of times I have heard operational staff and clients say they feel quite removed and disconnected from their organisation's overarching purpose gives me pause for deep contemplation. In many cases, I have found these people don't know or care very much about what is in the strategic plan. I have also encountered situations where no-one outside senior management knows what is in the organisation's strategic plan because it is a document that cannot be disclosed to other people due to privacy concerns. In some cases, people candidly tell me the only reason they have a strategic plan is to comply with what the standards for their industry or sector require. I have also been told that working on any aspect of a strategic plan is irrelevant and takes staff away from the important work do with their clients.

At the same time, I hold a sense of excitement when I think about the energy and vibrancy that is obvious when organisations have a long-term strategy that is linked to a strong societal purpose – not just for the organisation in general, but also for each person working for the organisation. Similarly, the considerations about how technology can actively support people to do their work can be motivating and inspiring to hear. While not yet a common approach with the services I audit, there is a very different 'vibe' to what is being developed, actioned and achieved when this is the approach taken by organisations and businesses that courageously face a different type of future.

Some of the most profound and deeply sustainable changes have occurred in organisations and businesses when judgement and fear about what is possible have been suspended, and different ideas and options have been given an opportunity to be examined and to be trialled. Where I have seen this done in organisations, efforts were made to involve *every* person working for or involved with the organisation, not just those at senior management and governance levels. In many of these cases, the board organised external facilitators or futurists to work with people and encourage the contribution of ideas and possible solutions for the way ahead.

Sometimes these ideas initially look quite bizarre and a bit wacky, but as people seriously considered the ways these ideas could affect their organisation, their thinking often expanded and other ideas came forward. For example, actively marketing the business via apps where clients could easily do a cost comparison among different organisations for their specific requirements, or using different forms of technology in client's homes and linking this back to apps that can be viewed elsewhere. What is striking in these situations is the courage displayed by the board or business owner in suspending their own ideas and judgement, and being open to hearing and then analysing completely different points of view to take the organisation forward.

Considerations for the audits of the future

As clients approach organisations and businesses for services and supports as a result of using apps and different forms of technology to make their decisions, organisations might find this change to be disruptive and uncomfortable if they continue to use outdated service delivery methods that might be better suited to the past. Similarly, auditors need to be up to date and across the different technologies being used by organisations.

Audits and assessments conducted remotely from an organisation's location are becoming more common, with the result being that auditors will be expected to continually adapt to the changing world of technology and how these changes impact the business environment. Other factors that auditors need to consider include:

> ➤ The role of 'soft skills' and emotional intelligence[34] such as:

- the ability to retain rapport with people when an audit or assessment is undertaken with the use of technology
- being able to express empathy and be self-aware, self-regulated and adaptable in a tight schedule
- being aware of their attitude, work ethic and team-working capabilities
- maintaining and actively using creative as well as critical thinking skills
- maintaining positivity, motivation and appropriate use of humour
- time management skills
- conflict management skills.

> The ability to develop expansive seeing.[35] This means seeing beyond things that are directly in front of them. For example, there are many more components to an organisation than only one program, one outcome, one success, one point in time or one crisis. Auditors need to think about how they see the system, especially when the audit is undertaken remotely.

> The equipment they use. For example, having computers and other technology, such as smartphones that interface and work together to enable the auditor to view evidence in different formats and on different devices. Making sure the equipment is constantly charged is important, as is adequate internet coverage and the ability to rapidly go online when needed.

> Being aware of the equipment used by the organisation or business. For example, do they have separate devices that can be used by staff for the duration of the audit or assessment? What happens if there is not enough

equipment or capacity for staff to use the equipment? Is the organisation able to readily access the internet?

> The time taken to change to different forms of technology or to bring people into online meetings. Often there is a lag period as different types of technology are being set up or practices transferred between one technology and another. This can have an unexpected effect on the timeframes for different activities in the audit or assessment plan.

> The impact on the audit team, particularly when juggling different activities on the plan from different locations, and being mindful of not doubling up on the use of an organisation's equipment for specific timeslots on the audit plan.

> The impact of fatigue associated with intense concentration, particularly with managing technology in reviewing and analysing evidence – for both auditor and organisation staff.

> The requirement for the auditor to rapidly acquire skills, knowledge and the ability to manage very different forms of technology between one organisation and the next.

> Being mindful of working with organisations and businesses that are also managing significant internal turmoil or the impact of external natural disasters as well as managing the practicalities associated with the audit or assessment.

As Robert F Kennedy and other famous people have said, '*We live in interesting times*' – and it would be fair to say that we are also right in the thick of the most creative time in human history, where anything is possible.

Reflections

How prepared are you to adjust to using rapidly changing technology within an audit structure?

....

....

....

....

In what ways do you work with organisations to prepare them for audits using technology?

....

....

....

....

What are the potential impacts on organisations when they purchase 'off-the-shelf' policy manuals and expect to achieve certification based on the manual content?

....

....

....

....

How do you manage 'soft skills' and the ability to establish and maintain rapport with staff in an organisation when an audit is conducted remotely?

....

....

....

....

....

....

How do you manage to maintain your critical thinking within a fast-paced audit environment?

....

....

....

....

....

....

....

12.

WHAT NEEDS TO CHANGE

It's not the strongest that survive, nor the most intelligent, but those most responsive to change.
(ATTRIBUTED TO CHARLES DARWIN)

Stepping up to the changes ...

In over a decade of auditing and assessing work, I have rarely heard anyone – anywhere – say that any audit, including their own, is an inspirational exercise. Similarly, I rarely hear people say they are enthusiastically looking forward to their next audit. Most people I know would say that if people were looking forward to an audit, there must be something wrong with them!

In contrast to the traditional view of audits and assessments being a 'necessary evil', I wonder what the world would be like if audits and assessments were inspirational and a valued component of an organisation's business strategy? While we are hearing more and more about the role of digital tools in workplaces and the rise of artificial intelligence, discussions are also occurring about the impact of these technologies on the auditor's work throughout the 2020s.

We don't appear to be able to halt the march of technological progress – nor would we want to – but there is an increasing need to accelerate human development at this time.[36] In particular, humans need to have an increased capacity to manage moral and ethical complexities in the workplace, in the community and in relationships with other people.

The search for improvements in auditing practice

Reflecting on the wide array of research that has been conducted into auditing as well as auditor practice over the past couple of decades, it seems to me that the world is searching for improvements to the way audits and assessments function and operate. In particular, we are seeking improvements that have substance, and are more than a surface solution when dealing with increasingly complex systemic situations. This is the case whether a business or organisation is large, small, global or local.

The focus appears to be more on changes in practices that need to occur 'out there' and outside of ourselves. It would be fair to say that we can develop a sound understanding of theory but don't always appreciate that change has to come from ourselves as well.

Frequently, the first steps towards change have to come from within. We need to do our internal work and grapple with what the changes mean and how they 'fit' – not only with our beliefs, but also in how we enable ourselves to move forward with these ideals and a new sense of purpose. From my research and discussions with people, there doesn't appear to be any acknowledgement that the improvements have to come from us first – and this includes in our role as an auditor. We have to step up and be better at what we are doing.

Over the years, much has been written about the skills and attributes required of professional quality auditors and assessors. A logical response would be to develop checklists itemising the auditor's required skills and attributes and to engage only auditors with those characteristics.

The search for something more ...

While a good auditor gets things done, a *great* auditor aspires, inspires and achieves more through an unwavering resolve to do what must be done. As Jim Collins says – though not necessarily about the world of auditors or assessors – 'Good is the enemy of great.'[37] However, the reality is that it can be difficult to find people with 'something more' who can step up or have the capacity to become a great auditor or assessor.

From what I can see, having 'something more' for today's auditors means being people with influence, credibility, standing and a sound reputation within their own industries and sectors. They have the ability to learn from both positive and negative feedback and continually seek to understand themselves more deeply as well as learn about best practice methods that can build up the organisations and businesses they audit and assess.

In many ways, they are the ambassadors of the auditing realms. They are the people who truly live and breathe what being an inspirational auditor is all about.

Level 5: Ambassador Auditor

*Excellence is to do a common thing
in an uncommon way.*
(BOOKER T WASHINGTON)

LEVELS	TYPE	FOCUS	POSITION	RESULT	VALUE
LEVEL 5	AMBASSADOR	LEVERAGE	INFLUENCER	STRENGTH	+90%+
LEVEL 4	EXPERT	INSIGHT	PRODUCER	VALUE	+70%
LEVEL 3	LEAD	COMPLIANCE	GUIDE	ASSURANCE	+40%
LEVEL 2	SUPPORT	COMPETENCE	CONTRIBUTOR	ASSISTANCE	-10%
LEVEL 1	NOVICE	SYSTEM	FOLLOWER	INVISIBLE	-20%

Ambassador Auditors encourage and, in fact, call upon CEOs and their organisations to step up and demonstrate best practice, not only with their governance practices, but also through focused attention on the internal and external clients as well as on strategies that strengthen the organisation and its business activities.

One of the strengths of an Ambassador Auditor as a systems leader is the ability to see the larger system.[38] Most people, including many Lead Auditors, typically place their attention on the parts of the system right in front of them, or the areas where they know the most about how things should work. This can result in people striving to be right in any given situation or argument, with attention subsequently taken away from what is happening within and across the larger system.

As a systems leader, an Ambassador Auditor helps people to see the larger system and the various ways the different sections work together to achieve an organisation's bigger purpose. Sometimes this approach requires Ambassador Auditors to provide insights and details leading to a shared understanding of the different parts of the larger system. However, underlying these insights is the continued motivation to strive for high quality while being instinctively aware that they must take responsibility when the standard of their own work falls short of expectations.

People working at this level understand and appreciate the level of quality needed to deliver audit outcomes that give confidence and assurances to organisations.

Ambassador Auditors frequently ask questions such as:

What will be my contribution to strengthening and improving each business or organisation I audit?

> What will I do to make sure people are placed first in every audit situation?
> What do I do to make sure a moral and ethical foundation underpins my work?
> What do I need to do to make sure every person I meet in any audit is treated as a human being with inalienable rights?
> What kind of outcomes do I want to see as a result of my auditing work with organisations and businesses?
> What do I need to do to be the best version of myself – all of the time?

The internal work that Ambassador Auditors do

The unexamined life is not worth living.
(SOCRATES)

In order to achieve high-level outcomes, Ambassador Auditors frequently employ courageous communication techniques to explore and, where possible, expose blind spots that could be detrimental to an organisation's or business's progress. At the same time, they are aware of their own blind spots and courageously face these within their work.

How often have we heard people say things like, '*If only someone had told me about my tendency to fixate on irrelevant minutiae five years ago, I could have done something about it*'? Perhaps we were not able to hear or acknowledge any situations where minor faults were pointed out to us at the time, and we are now living with much bigger problems that could have been avoided if we had listened to what other people – preferably trusted people – were pointing out to us.

Sometimes our reactions can be so strong that other people subsequently decide to not tell us what the impacts of our behaviours or attitudes are on them. This can result in people 'walking on eggshells' and being afraid to point out what we may have been doing wrong.

There is no one right way of developing an understanding about blind spots, and frequently it can feel like being in a confronting *Groundhog Day*[39] situation until lessons are learned, the traditional ways of thinking and acting are broken, and we can go forward again. The reality is everyone has blind spots: those aspects of ourselves, our behaviour and our attitudes that we do not know or understand, yet can be seen clearly and explained by other people. Sometimes we react when other people point out some of these aspects to us and may not believe the observations have any truth to them. However, many Ambassador Auditors have the ability to seek out their blind spots and incorporate the acquired knowledge into their work, not only for themselves, but for the people they work with in audit or assessment situations.

What makes an Ambassador Auditor stand out from the rest?

I am personally convinced that one person can be a change catalyst, a 'transformer' in any situation, any organization. Such an individual is yeast that can leaven an entire loaf. It requires vision, initiative, patience, respect, persistence, courage and faith to be a transforming leader.

(STEPHEN R COVEY)

From a foundation of a deep understanding about themselves and their craft as an auditor, Ambassador Auditors are catalysts for change. Their work in any audit or assessment often introduces new knowledge and insights that can be used to strengthen an organisation's business operations.

The term 'catalyst' refers to a person or thing that precipitates an event' and, by the very nature of an Ambassador Auditor's involvement within an audit process, changes often do occur, whether the Ambassador Auditor is aware of these changes or not at the time.

Being a catalyst for change is not an unusual function for an Ambassador Auditor. However, the *choice* to become a catalyst and to develop particular leadership skills is the responsibility and calling of the individual: it is not something that can be imposed on people. It is something that the individual learns – and *leans into* – over time. This means the individual learns how to manage uncertainty and appreciates the benefits of taking managed risks, along with developing deep skills that are refined through practice and the incorporation of learnings associated with failed as well as successful efforts in these areas.

Research suggests that the catalyst has a number of key beliefs.[40] These include:

> ➤ an inherent faith in their ability to change and improve their environment
> ➤ the certainty that learning is a key task to be accomplished in the process
> ➤ a belief in the benefits of mutual influence
> ➤ actively engaging others in a joint search for solutions.

It all comes back to the individual's mindset, which basically includes a set of beliefs and a way of looking at and thinking about the world as well as of their place in it. In her work on mindsets, Carol Dweck has observed that the types of beliefs most noticeable in people who operate as a catalyst constitute a 'growth mindset'.[41] For Ambassador Auditors, this approach incorporates a deep-seated and fundamental commitment towards the growth and strengthening of an organisation's capacity to address its fundamental purpose, evident not only during the audit process, but also looking to the future and what needs to be changed and evolved to serve the needs of clients over time.

But consciously taking on the role of catalyst or change agent is far from an easy proposition for an Ambassador Auditor. Efforts to facilitate an organisation's own awareness of the need for change, whether in systems or individuals, can lead to great frustration for an Ambassador Auditor if they are not careful. These auditors are certainly aware of their responsibility for change, but not for *all* of it – particularly when the changes are being considered and implemented (or not) by the organisations and businesses being audited. Ambassador Auditors frequently monitor the consciousness of an organisation before delving deeply into options that complement and enhance the focus of its audit. Because of their level of influence and mastery of audit and business practices, Ambassador Auditors can find that other people's lives are changed in ways they could never imagine.

Having some semblance of personal awareness as well as a deep understanding about where and how their personal beliefs and biases can affect situations and individuals are important considerations for Ambassador Auditors.

From what I have seen of Ambassador Auditors, they assume the role and responsibilities of catalyst[42] or change agent and are very mindful of their ability to:[43]

> ➤ operate with integrity and consideration, honour their word, do what is expected even when they haven't explicitly agreed to do more than the basics[44]
> ➤ operate with a strong sense of purpose and a focus on social good

> be an intuitive listener, sensing things that other people
  don't.

They are also known for:

> walking the talk, talking the walk *and* walking it like they
  talk it
> peer leadership
> routinely using authentic presence
> high-level commitment towards the value of lifelong
  learning, continuity of seeking knowledge and
  maintaining intellectual curiosity
> high-level diplomatic practice, walking people through
  challenging situations
> deep change management skills – acknowledging the
  catalyst role
> seeing the higher-level vision as well as observations and
  possibilities for the business or organisation
> high levels of personal integrity, commitment and
  congruence
> working with a 'gut feel' and intuition
> respectfully challenging the status quo, when
  needed
> effectively using challenging, creative and open-minded
  thinking
> high levels of versatility, tenacity, accountability and the
  ability to give credit where it is due
> excellence in communication (e.g. rapidly developing
  rapport, providing clear explanations of concepts and
  details, making ethical considerations, educating and
  guiding people during stressful times)

> high stamina and resilience levels – plus high levels of self-care
> rapidly and flexibly moving into a new direction as well as drawing on professional knowledge and detail, when needed.

In addition, they maintain a keen sense of self-awareness and alertness towards larger patterns and connections, while also aligning their auditing work into a vocation with purpose and vision. The Ambassador Auditors I have seen certainly appear to view life's challenges and adversity within a context of personal and spiritual growth,[45] even if it is not always explained that way.

What does this mean for organisations and businesses?

Going forward, organisations and businesses will expect to be more selective about the auditors and assessors that conduct personable yet professional audits – either onsite or remotely. They may also have stronger expectations about the auditor's personal and professional principles.

At the same time, auditors and assessors that step up and actively engage in high-level auditing practices undertake actions that:

> help people to love what they hate
> help them to see and do what they believe they can't
> provide encouragement
> provide assistance
> reinforce people's successes

> encourage better practices so that good behaviour is made easier and poor behaviour is made harder.[46]

*Be the change you want to
see in the world.*
(GANDHI)

Isn't it time we made this happen?

Reflections

Do you know of anyone who is an Ambassador Auditor? What makes them stand out from other auditors?

....
....
....
....
....
....
....

In what ways can you see Ambassador Auditors being the change they want to see in the world? Is this important?

....
....
....
....
....
....
....
....

If you aspire to be an Ambassador Auditor, what steps do you need to take now?

....

....

....

....

....

....

....

In what ways do you continually examine your own auditing practice? What happens if you don't do this?

....

....

....

....

....

....

....

....

13.

THE NEXT STEPS ...

Be a yardstick of quality. Some people aren't used to an environment where excellence is expected.
(STEVE JOBS)

So, what needs to be done now? How can Lead Auditors and Expert Auditors become even better at what they do? What difference will that make?

I think it is time for the world to see the benefits associated with auditors who have taken their expertise further into the realm of influence, inspiration, impact and mastery. In auditing and assessing organisations and businesses, we cannot continue to use the 'same old, same old' auditing practices and expect to be relevant in a world that is progressing rapidly into the 4th Industrial Revolution.

We need to develop a new attitude to our auditing practice. This will result not only in a new attitude in the way in which we work and operate but also an ongoing foundation for further development and refinement of our aptitude.

In this new environment, there are many opportunities to

look at refining and valuing the role of auditing and assessing. For auditors, regardless of skill level, there is a requirement to courageously step up and be open about what we know – and what we don't know – as we work together to strengthen the purpose and focus of organisations and businesses within an improved auditing framework.

∞

This book covers a lot of the steps for an auditor to consider on their journey: from the stages of thinking about auditing as a career through to the initial practices for Novices Auditors and on to attaining the level of Ambassador Auditor. The concepts described in this book are designed to help you think about the reasons why you want to be an auditor, where you are now and what is next for you.

The ideas presented here are designed to help you consider your auditing role far more deeply than you may have before. The focus on compliance is only one part of what you do as an auditor. There are so many opportunities to build upon what you know and to make a real difference to the organisations and businesses you audit.

The key for you to remember is that all auditors, regardless of who they are and their level of practice, started somewhere. It is important for you to feel encouraged and motivated to take your own steps towards being the best auditor you can be. Our world needs auditors who think beyond a solely compliance-focused, checklist-oriented mindset. We need auditors who can coura- geously stand up and conduct audits that help organisations meet their purpose and vision, not only for their current clients, but also for the people who will need these services and businesses beyond 2030. You can truly make a difference! What that looks like is really up to you.

Do not go where the path may lead. Go instead where there is no path and leave a trail.
(RALPH WALDO EMERSON)

ABOUT KATHY REES

As a longstanding auditor and assessor, Kathy Rees brings her wide-ranging experience with directing and managing companies and services in the disability and human services sectors into her work. She is not interested in a standard 'tick-box' audit or assessment; instead, her passion is in strengthening the 'back of house' functions of an organisation so that it is better equipped to meet the needs of its clients, regardless of who they are or what they require.

Kathy uses her knowledge and experience to work with organisations that aim to meet – and exceed – the Human Services Quality Standards and NDIS Practice Standards as well as ISO 9001:2015. This approach extends to her experience on the other side of the table in preparing for the audits of her Registered Training Organisation, as well as the audits of the service she managed for her disabled daughter for over twenty years.

Kathy works with people who are interested in auditing as a career, as well as those who want further guidance as they commence on their auditor journey. She helps people to understand what is actually involved with being a professional and respected auditor and spends time demystifying the types of practices that the auditor will need to implement along the way.

She is a speaker at conferences and seminars, and runs workshops on auditing practices for people who want to know more. Kathy is an avid researcher and project manager who believes that an auditor's humour, optimism and stewardship actively contribute towards purposeful outcomes for the organisations that they audit.

To request more information about how you can work with Kathy or have her speak at your next event, please email: admin@onlyaboutquality.com

You can access Kathy Rees Author Page via this link: www.onlyaboutquality.com/book

www.onlyaboutquality.com

LinkedIn.com: https://www.linkedin.com/in/kathyrees/

ACKNOWLEDGEMENTS

Without a phone call out of the blue from Scott Douglas and a subsequent meeting with Scott and Suzanne Le Huray from HDAA Australia Pty Ltd in 2010, I would not have commenced down the pathway to become an auditor and subsequent assessor, and this book would not have been written. Amazing how these two events have changed my life!

While the process for writing this book began early in 2020, the ideas were forming long before then. I commenced Jane Anderson's Women with Influence program in 2018 and without her encouragement I would not have had the courage to write a book such as this one. So, a huge thank you to Jane and the Women with Influence colleagues who have supported me along the way.

To Brian Amos who was instrumental in showing me what a courageous auditor actually does, my immense thanks and gratitude. Brian, along with Katrina Johnson from NewSky Consulting and Lyne Mear from Lyne Mear and Associates were the readers of my first manuscript and each one has contributed so much more to my thinking and writing journey than they will ever know. Katrina also provided much-valued assistance with the diagrams in this book. Her encouragement, not only for the book, but also for what goes along with it, have meant a lot to me.

Special gratitude goes to David Hamer and Suzanne Le Huray at HDAA Australia Pty Ltd, who have continually and enthusiastically supported my auditing journey as well as the intent of what I wanted to achieve with this book. And a big shout out to David as well. Right from the beginning of my auditing journey, he provoked my thinking about the roles of auditors and assessors and what we can really *do* for the organisations, businesses and services we work with in this arena. I am looking forward to many more fruitful discussions in the years ahead, David!

Next, a big thank you to Dixie Carlson and her amazing team at Indie Experts – this book would definitely not have come together without your incredible input and encouragement. Dixie helped me to understand what is involved in being an author, which, as it turns out, is far more than just writing a book. Many thanks too to Ann Dettori Wilson for guiding me with the production of the book and for patiently helping me to see what needed to be done. I am hugely, deeply appreciative for the input provided by Kaaren Sutcliffe in the second editorial review. Kaaren's own experience as an auditor was incredibly helpful, particularly through her own questions and insights that helped me to be very clear about what I was saying.

Thank you too to my virtual assistant Julie Crouch from Integral Virtual Services, who has helped me so much with formulating my newsletters and blogs. She has made sense of and refined what I have written about the role of the auditor over the past year.

Much gratitude to the people involved in the significantly amended scenarios (to protect their privacy) that I used throughout the book. You helped to shape my thinking about the value that auditing can have on strengthening organisations over time. As far as I am concerned, nothing beats people saying how excited they are about seeing me again and wanting to show off all that they have developed and implemented in the period since their last audit!

The biggest thank you goes to my children Belinda, Tracy and Ben, who continually inspire me in their own very different ways. You are amazing and the world is a better place for you being in it!

REFERENCES

1   Forbes Insights (2015). *Audit 2020: A Focus on Change* [online] https://www.forbes.com/forbesinsights/kpmg_audit/index. html (accessed 14.2.2019).

2   Bonner, S. & Pennington, N. (1991). Cognitive Processes and Knowledge as Determinants of Auditor Expertise, *Journal of Accounting Literature*, Vol 10, pp1–50.

3   Russell, J. (editor) (2013). *The ASQ Auditing Handbook* (4th edition). ASQ. p138.

4   Op cit iii p138.

5   Op cit i (accessed 14.2.2019).

6   Anderson, A. W. (2012). The Characteristics of a Successful Auditor [online] https://www.kscpa.org/writable/files/Self-Study/AAE/12._aae_self-study.pdf (accessed 14.2.2019).

7   Wahid, R., Grigg, N., & Prajogo, D. (2019) Auditor Education for the 21st Century: A Delphi Study, conducted by the Universiti of Teknologi Mara (Malaysia), Massey University (New Zealand) and Monash University (Australia).

8   Forbes Insights (2017). *Audit 2025: The Future Is Now* [online] https://www.forbes.com/forbesinsights/kpmg_audit2025/ index.html (accessed 18.2.2019).

9   Bautista Smith, J. (2012). *Auditing Beyond Compliance*, ASQ.

10   Forbes Insights (2017). *Audit 2025: The Future Is Now* [online] https://www.forbes.com/forbesinsights/kpmg_audit2025/index.html (accessed 18.2.2019).

11   Covey, S. (1989). *The Seven Habits of Highly Effective People*, Free Press.

12   Goleman, D. (2005). *Emotional Intelligence: Why It Can Matter More than IQ*, Bantam Publishers.

13   Yang, L., Brink, A., & Wier, B. (2018). The Impact of Emotional Intelligence on Auditor Judgement, *International Journal of Auditing*, Volume 22, Issue 1, pp83–97.

14   Gerber, M. (2004). *The E-Myth Revisited*, Harper Business.

15   The Health Foundation. (2010). *Evidence Scan: Complex Adaptive Systems* [online] https://www.health.org.uk/sites/default/files/ComplexAdaptiveSystems.pdf (accessed 3.3.2020).

16   Freud, S. [online] https://medium.com/achology/the-three-levels-of-human-consciousness-6d9a59fed577 and https://open textbc.caintroductiontopsychology/chapter/2-2-psycho dynamic-and-behavioural-psychology/

17   KPMG. (2018). *Global CEO Outlook 2018: Australia* [online] https://home.kpmg/au/en/home/insights/2018/05/global-ceo-outlook-2018-australia.html (accessed 18.2.2019).

18   *Human Services Quality Framework: The Current and Future Landscape*, Day 2 – Auditor Training, 18.1.2019, Brisbane

19   Forbes Insights (2017). *Audit 2025: The Future Is Now* [online] https://www.forbes.com/forbesinsights/kpmg_audit2025/index.html (accessed 18.2.2019).

20   Hutton, D. (1994). *The Change Agent's Handbook: A Survival Guide for Quality Improvement Champions*, ASQC Quality Press.

21   Deloitte Access Economics. (2016). *Forecasting the Future in Community Services In Queensland 2025* [online] https://

www2.deloitte.com/content/dam/Deloitte/au/Documents/ Economics/deloitte-au-forecasting-future-community-servic- es-qld-010416.pdf (accessed 18.2.2019).

22 Forbes Insights (2017). *Audit 2025: The Future Is Now* [online] https://www.forbes.com/forbesinsights/kpmg_audit2025/ index.html (accessed 18.2.2019).

23 Forbes Insights (2015). *Audit 2020: A Focus on Change* [online] https://www.forbes.com/forbesinsights/kpmg_audit/index. html (accessed 14.2.2019).

24 Coleman, L. (2015). *Advanced Quality Auditing*, ASQ.

25 Ryall, J. (2019). AOQ President's Message, *Quality Business*, Issue 1, p4.

26 Fountaine, T., McCarthy, B., & Saleh, T. (2019). Building the AI-Powered Organisation, *Harvard Business Review*, July/ August 2019, pp62–73.

27 Verint Research (2019). *Engagement in the Always-On Era: How human and technology work hand-in-hand to meet rising expectations* [online] https://www.verint.com/gb/research/ research-paper/ (accessed 2.3.2020).

28 Schwab, K. (2017). *The Fourth Industrial Revolution*, Penguin Random House.

29 Forbes Insights (2017). *Audit 2025: The Future Is Now* [online] https://www.forbes.com/forbesinsights/kpmg_audit2025/ index.html (accessed 18.2.2019).

30 Hoggett, E., Dubois, S., O'Connor, S., & Jamieson, R. (2019). Improving Audit Quality with New Technology. *KPMG* [online] https://home.kpmg/au/en/home/insights/2019/02/ audit-technology-future-technology-audit-quality.html (accessed 2.3.2020).

31 Rispin, C. (2009). *How to Think Like A Futurist: Know First, Be First, Profit First*, The Future Trends Group.

32   Rees, K. (2013). It's not just about the support: Exploring the ways in which family members and people with disabilities evaluate their self-directed/self-managed arrangements (NDIS research through the Practical Design Fund and FaHCSIA) [online] https://www.slideshare.net/KathyRees1/ndispdfreport21042013-49202480.

33   McQueen, M. (2013). *Winning the Battle for Relevance: Why Even the Greatest Become Obsolete and How to Avoid Their Fate*, Nexgen Group.

34   Goleman, D. (2005). *Emotional Intelligence: Why It Can Matter More Than IQ*, Bantam Publishers.

35   Hacker, S. K. & Washington, M. (2018). *Lead Self First Before Leading Others: A Life Planning Resource*, Business Expert Press.

36   Howard, A. (2015). *Humanise: Why Human-Centred Leadership is the Key to the 21st Century*, Wiley.

37   Collins, J. (2001). *Good to Great: Why some companies make the leap ... and others don't*, Random House Business.

38   Senge, P., Hamilton, H., & Kanis, J. (2015). The Dawn of System Leadership, *Stanford Social Innovation Review*, Volume 13, Number 1, p14.

39   See, for example, https://www.quora.com/What-is-the-symbolism-behind-the-movie-%E2%80%9CGroundhog-Day%E2%80%9D and https://transparencynow.com/groundhog.htm to explain the purpose for repetition in the movie, 'Groundhog Day', and its impact on the lead character over time.

40   Liedtka, J., Rosen, R., & Wiltbank, R. (2009). *The Catalyst: How You Can Become an Extraordinary Growth Leader*, Crown Business. p38.

41   Dweck, C. (2006). *Mindset: The New Psychology of Success*, Random House.

42   Maxwell, J. (2016). *The 17 Indisputable Laws of Teamwork: Embrace Them and Empower Your Team*, Thomas Nelson.

43   Liedtka, J., Rosen, R., & Wiltbank, R. (2009). *The Catalyst: How You Can Become an Extraordinary Growth Leader*, Crown Business.

44   Zaffron, S. & Logan, D. (2009). *The Three Laws of Performance: Rewriting the Future of Your Organisation and Your Life*, Jossey-Bass.

45   Zohar, D. (1997). *ReWiring the Corporate Brain: Using the New Science to Rethink How We Structure and Lead Organizations*, Berrett-Koehler.

46   Grenny, J., Patterson, K., Maxfield, D., McMillan, R., & Switzler, A. (2013). *Influencer: The New Science of Leading Change*, McGraw-Hill Education.